I MET THE HUMBLED CHRIST IN RUSSIA

A PILGRIM IN THE SOVIET UNION

by

Rev. Emile Briere
Priest of Madonna House

With an Introductory Poem and an Appendix by
Catherine de Hueck Doherty
Founder of Madonna House

DIMENSION BOOKS, INC.

Denville, New Jersey

First Edition

Published by Dimension Books, Inc.

Copyright © 1976 by Emile Briere

CONTENTS

INTRODUCTION

Today, millions of people travel. Tourism is an international phenomenon. Feverishly we run here and there in pursuit of happiness, excitement and novelty. Whether we know it or not, we are really seeking the Absolute in all this fun and frolic, the only One who can give us real happiness. The pilgrim is simply a person who consciously knows and acknowledges this. Of set purpose, the pilgrim seeks the Absolute in his travels.

What is a pilgrim? Listen to one who knows from experience. The following words were written by Catherine de Hueck Doherty (nee Catherine de Kolyschkine). She was born of Russian-Polish ancestry, in Leningrad, at the turn of our century. In 1930 she founded Friendship House in Toronto; a similar House was established in Harlem, N.Y., in 1938. In 1947 she began a new work, the Madonna House Apostolate in Combermere, Ontario, Canada. She has been a pilgrim all her life, and these words flow from her pilgrimage:

I am a pilgrim of the Lord.
I walk the earth and sing of Heaven!
I have no silver, nor do I carry any gold—
Yet, I am rich in wine and oil
That heal the wounded, lonely, and blind.

I have no home, yet in my heart there is an inn
That can expand to take the world in.

5

THE HUMBLED CHRIST IN RUSSIA

I know the darkness of the night—
Yet I walk in the Lord's noon light.
The noon-day devils walk at my side from morn to night—
But they can't touch me
For the Queen of Pilgrims walks with me.

I am a pilgrim of the Lord.
Heat, cold, hunger are my lot.
A sinner I, yet one who can and must carry the sins of others.
A pilgrim of the Lord am I.
A beggar who can dispense love with a joyous heart—
For love fills me daily with its bread and wine!

I am a pilgrim of the Lord
Who walks and prays the simple "Jesus prayer" all the day—
Beseeching Father, Son, and Holy Ghost
To make all men one in Them!

I wend my way
From holy shrine to holy shrine,
Bringing the sins of men and mine—
And laying them in the hands of Mercy—again, again!

I am a pilgrim of the Lord.
Love drives me on and on—to love, to pray, and to atone.
I am a pilgrim of the Lord.

Why cannot we turn all our traveling into pilgrimages? Make explicit what is already deep in our hearts? This is the story of my pilgrimage to Russia, a land nobody knows.

Special thanks to my dear friend, Father Bob Wild, of the Madonna House family, for editing the manuscript and for making many helpful suggestions.

E. Briere
Madonna House
March, 1975

1. THE CROSS OF PEACE AND LOVE

My trip through the Soviet Union was a dream come true, due to the generosity and kindness of many friends. I wanted to carry back to Russia the cross of *Pax-Caritas* (peace and love), the cross which members of our community wear and which has brought so much warmth and light to so many people, not only in North America but throughout the world. This cross had been shaped in that vast country during the early days of our century by the Holy Spirit and by the Bogoroditza (she-who-gave-birth-to-God) in the heart of Catherine Doherty, the foundress of Madonna House Apostolate. I wore that cross for a month, blessing the streets of many Russian cities, blessing the land which is so holy and dear to every Russian heart, blessing each person among the thousands who crossed my path.

One thing about Russians, they react. They have a habit of taking you in at a glance. They notice symbols, for many of them wear some kind of lapel button or insignia. Thousands saw the *Pax-Caritas* cross. Most of them reacted favorably to it, with a smile or a little inclination of the head, a bow of understanding. Some expressed annoyance. A few growled. Two or three cursed. But all reacted, which reveals indubitably that God still matters to them, they are involved with him, they love him, they hate him, they are either hot or cold, but not indifferent, tepid or lukewarm.

My lasting impression was of a people very much alive, strong, eager, proud of who they are, conscious of their mysterious destiny. They may be a mystery to us, but they are also a mystery to themselves. They are full of contradictions. They profess to be atheists or agnostics, to have rejected God. All this they proclaim loudly with many gestures and many words while passing by a renovated church and gazing upon it with reverence.

After the 1917 revolution the vast majority of churches were used as factories, warehouses and workshops. Many of their icons were splintered for kindling wood. Today, the most common sight in Russia around many of these churches is *scaffolding*. They are being restored to their original grace and beauty. It is strange to associate with people who claim to be materialists, enthusiastic only for earthly progress, while at the same time gazing upon a golden cupola or a cross rising in the distance. Rarely in the Soviet Union does your eye not rest upon a church dome or an angel topping a column or a saint holding up a cross. It was a great joy for me to bless Catherine's homeland with the very cross God had given her to bless my own homeland!

I felt a great affinity with the Russian people and with Russia itself. We Canadians also carry in our veins the mysterious charm of mountains, where the heart spontaneously praises God. We have vast prairies which extend like an ocean, where men can dream dreams. We have forests, lakes and rivers which foster the spirit of adventure in men. There is the stark, immense northland, a challenge to one's courage and ingenuity.

Canada, too, is a mysterious country, and each Canadian carries in his subconscious that blend of praise, dreams and adventure which his land nurtured in him. I felt at home indeed with Russians and in Russia. The language barrier presented no difficulty whatsoever. I felt at home because of my Canadian background, but especially because of my close association for over thirty years with a very great Russian woman, Catherine de Hueck Doherty.

Something in my heart wanted to walk that land in the company of the humiliated Christ, of Our Lady of

Vladimir, of St. Nicholas, and of the millions of pilgrims who had gone on so many journeys to so many shrines to atone for the sins of all mankind. I wanted to be present to the risen Lord who lives in every person, be he atheist, saint or sinner. The Russian saints had taught me not to judge or to make distinctions among people, not to categorize them, not to divide them into good and bad.

When Christ was revealed to the Russians in the tenth century, they were moved to love and adore the *suffering* Christ. They loved and adored him in every suffering brother or sister. They quickly acquired a special fondness for the rejects of society: the criminals (whom they actually called the suffering ones, the cross bearers), the drunks, the prostitutes, the homosexuals, the serfs bereft of all rights. In their estimation, these were the people especially dear to the Lord Jesus Christ. The Russian saints honored them, reverenced them; tenderness and gentleness went out to them as to the humiliated Christ himself who once again had taken flesh and suffered among men.

A pilgrim—as I was taught by these saints—has a clear and definite role to perform, a great privilege indeed: the joy of recognizing and greeting the humiliated Christ (the suffering Lord, *glorious* though suffering) in each person he meets. I did that. I recognized and loved the glorious-suffering Christ in my guides, my chauffeurs, the people who crossed my path on Nevsky Avenue in Leningrad, Gorki Street in Moscow, on Kreschatik Avenue in Kiev, on Lenin Street in Irkutsk, Siberia. A strange thing happened to me then. As I saw the glory of the suffering Christ in each person, I became aware of his presence in me and I spontaneously cried out "Lord Jesus, have mercy on me a sinner."

Sometimes, at table in a restaurant, or on a tour, I found the situation getting tense, my heart becoming hard, my Western mind categorizing people. After a while something in me, perhaps the Holy Spirit, would remind me, "You are not here to judge but to love. You are not here to condemn but to adore. You are not here to express your arrogance but to share in the glory and the sin of all." Then I would very simply and consciously revere Christ in the people who were there with me. I would ask for mercy upon *me*. Within a few minutes the whole atmosphere would change, and a certain peace, joy and relaxation would arise from our hearts.

When I returned home to Madonna House, I forgot for a while about being a pilgrim, about finding the suffering Christ in myself and in my brothers and sisters. One day I remembered that we are pilgrims upon earth, wherever we may be, whatever we may do. We are walking daily on our way to the parousia, on our way to the Father, on our way to eternal joy. As the Madonna House constitutions say, "The Apostolate and its members are pilgrims in this world proclaiming the second coming of Christ when all things will be restored to him. Like all Christian pilgrims, the members travel in poverty to find security only in Christ; journey in chastity to serve and love Christ in men; live in obedience to be concerned only with the will of God." The simple conviction came to me that I should begin to live out here what the Russian saints had taught me: to walk freely, unencumbered through each day, as a *pilgrim*; to worship and love each person and the glorious suffering Christ, who identifies himself with each; to love him and reverence him in myself; to cry out, "Jesus, mercy," for myself and all mankind.

The first icon to come to Russia from Constantinople was an icon of tenderness eventually named "Our Lady of Vladimir." Our Lady holds the Child very tenderly in her arms; but the Child—who is God the Son—encircles her neck with his little arms, and presses his cheek against her cheek, and gazes upon her *with even greater tenderness.*

This icon made a profound impression upon the first Russian Christians. It marked their spirituality forever. They see in it the immense tenderness of Mary, the person closest to God; they see in it the infinite tenderness of the Child for his mother, *of God for his creature.*

It is in that tenderness we have our being, we move, we live from day to day. Our true place in the world is set in the very heart of Love. We have nothing to fear. We are free of guilt and shame. Our sin is forgiven before we have committed it. God holds nothing against us. *His forgiveness is an ongoing, never-ending activity.* Just as the desecrated Russian churches are now being restored to their original grace, so also is God constantly renewing, repairing, restoring the most magnificent temple in the world, each human being. ("Grace," by the way, is the word which best describes a Russian church: it is graceful and grace-full, not domineering or overwhelming, but delightful and graceful like a young woman coming to maturity.)

In Russia your heart constantly hears the cries of millions: serfs, intellectuals, revolutionaries, saints, who suffer and suffered there. You are never unaware of concentration camps. Your spirit joins an immense choir of voices crying out "Lord have mercy, Lord have mercy, Lord have mercy." Suffering for the world has long been familiar to the Russian people. They are vaguely aware of their destiny, of God who has entered their lives. Whether they know it or not, they carry the cross of the Lord Jesus Christ. They are sealed in the depths of their being by the presence of God.

2. THE MOTHER OF ALL RUSSIAN CITIES

Thanks to God, my own travel agent and Intourist (USSR), everything had been arranged before I left Canada so that my pilgrimage would begin at the beginning: in the utterly beautiful city of Kiev, situated mostly on the right bank of the great Dnieper River. The capital of Soviet Ukraine and the "mother of all Russian cities," as it is called, is situated midway on the trade route between Scandinavia and Constantinople.

In this breathtaking atmosphere the Russian nation was born. The original inhabitants of Kiev had come from the Pamir Mountains in northern Tibet around 2,300 B.C. Many of them settled in the Priapet Marshes west of the Dnieper River. Around the fifth and sixth centuries they moved to Kiev and its environs. These Slavonic tribes gave birth eventually to three principal groups—the Ukrainians, the Byelo Russians and the Great Russians. Here Christianity was brought from Constantinople to the Slav people by their ruler, St. Vladimir, in the year 989. Here Russian monasticism was born. Here Boris and Gleb, without offering any resistance, were murdered by their own brother. These two young men, sons of Vladimir, were spontaneously canonized by the people, not as martyrs but as innocent lambs who, like Christ, offered no resistance to the butcher's knife. Interesting that the first saints recognized by the Russian Orthodox Church should be laymen. They are also venerated as saints by the Roman Catholic Church.

My heart thrilled with anticipation and joy as my Aeroflot plane began its descent into the Kiev airport. As we came out of the clouds, the first thing I noticed was the big haystacks dotting well-groomed fields. I thought of Catherine Doherty, who has such a profound admiration for well-rounded haystacks. The attendants at the customs showed me not only every courtesy but immediately inquired with interest about my visit to the Soviet Union. They were truly moved when I explained to them that the cross I wore symbolized Peace and Love (Mir y Lubov). One of them said, "That's right, peace and love, not peace and friendship. Not just in peace and friendship, but in peace and love."

The sun was shining as we drove the long distance from the airport to the city center where my hotel was located. It gave me a chance to admire the well-ordered forests and fields. As we entered the city I gasped with delight at the number and charm of its numerous parks. The upper town stands some three hundred feet above the Dnieper, a treasure grove of trees and hills and flowers. At least half the area is devoted to parks.

During the drive I remembered the Canadians of Ukrainian descent. I recalled my many Ukrainian friends in Western Canada whom I had come to know and love during our years of study in St. Joseph's Seminary, Edmonton, Alberta. I recalled my first Ukrainian friend, a beautiful girl who belonged to my "gang" when I was a young man. Ours had been a truly ecumenical and intercultural group. There were young people of Anglo-Saxon descent, English, Scottish, Irish, French Canadians, Ukrainians, a Russian, a couple of Jews, some Protestants, some Catholics, and the University's lone atheist. We took good care of him and did our best not to convert him. In those days it was quite a distinction to have an atheist as a friend. Nobody wanted to spoil that.

We used to spend Sundays together listening to symphonies and operas, reading poetry during the winter, dancing all through the Christmas season, and going on hikes when

13

the spring finally came. As the taxi sped toward Kiev, my most vivid memory was that of some twenty young people patiently waiting outside the Ukrainian Church on Easter morning for our Ukrainian friend to join us for the first hike and picnic of the season. I'm not sure that I had any great love for the Divine Liturgy that morning as we waited and waited and waited. We good Roman Catholics had attended the shortest Mass in town. We were ready to hit the trail by nine o'clock, but the Eastern Rite service went on and on. Finally, around two o'clock in the afternoon, our friend came out and we decided to eat our lunch right there on the church grounds. On that particular Easter Sunday little did we know, little did we realize that one day, like the emissaries of Vladimir to Constantinople, to the Church of Hagia Sophia, I, too, at a liturgy, would feel that I had been transported into heaven.

My arrival at the hotel created a bit of a stir, and no wonder. Here was this stranger in a black suit, wearing a silver cross and a funny collar with a white strip in front. Such a sight is rare anywhere outside the enclosure of an active or working church, that is, a church open to worship. During my month in Russia, I traveled some ten thousand miles and walked down many a street in about ten cities. *Not once* did I meet a priest or minister, local or foreign, in clerical clothes.

The tourist in the Soviet Union is well cared for by *Intourist*, the official tourist agency of the USSR. Intourist clerks and guides meet you at the point of arrival and drive you in a good taxi to your hotel. The Intourist hotels are quite satisfactory on the whole. In the lobby, Intourist clerks sit at various desks, each ready to assist you with one thing or another: train tickets, excursions, taxis, mail, currency exchange, etc. Whatever your needs or complaints, Intourist is available, willing and courteous. In these hotels the restaurants are first class, the food abundant, tasty and cheap. All over Russia, steak is your best buy. It comes in various cuts with oven-fried potatoes and two vegetables. I paid about $1.50 for steaks everywhere outside Leningrad and Moscow, where the prices are about one-third higher. The service is top notch, and at supper you are entertained by singers, an orchestra, instrumentalists, with Russian folk songs, rock and popular music of other nations, especially of America. The youth of the world, including Russia, is crazy about rock!

After supper I walked around the hotel saying the Jesus prayer, Mary's rosary, opening my heart to share the love and prayers which so many people had given to me before leaving Canada. It was Sunday, a day of rest all over Russia. Hundreds of couples, people of all ages, were milling up and down the square in front of my hotel, and on Kreschatik Boulevard, Kiev's main street, which is lined with shops. I walked quietly in the warm autumn air absorbing people, atmosphere, things. At busy intersections you cross the street underground. In the large Russian cities, there seems to be literally a whole other network of streets and subways below the surface. I immediately felt at home. Many people noticed the cross without hostility. One young man came up to me and managed to convey that he also believed in Christ, that he prayed to God. He was immensely delighted to have this short conversation with me.

I turned in early. It had been some 24 hours since I had slept in a bed, but by two o'clock I was awake, too excited to sleep, at the prospect of visiting my dear friend, St. Theodosius, at the cave monastery that very morning. I offered Mass in my room. Slowly the prayer seemed to cover the whole of Kiev and tenderly embrace the whole of Russia.

The breakfast room opens at 8 o'clock in all hotels. There I enjoyed a healthy breakfast with a group of

American tourists. We had apple juice, two eggs, black and white bread, butter, jam, coffee. After breakfast, right in the hotel lobby, I was able to buy postcards and airmail stamps, to write the cards, mail them and exchange one hundred dollars for seventy-five rubles. At ten o'clock a Japanese Professor of English and I were met by our own special guide, Tamara, a fine university student. We drove off to visit the cave monastery, officially known as the Kiev-Pecharsky (cave) Lavra Monastery. It was founded in the eleventh century by St. Anthony, a monk from Mount Athos, and developed by St. Theodosius, a Kievan who is indeed the father of Russian monasticism.

I entered the monastery grounds—about fifty acres and some eighty buildings—by the gate-Church of the Trinity. Gate-churches are common in Russia. All monasteries served at times as fortresses and were surrounded by a thick protective wall. Here the officials and people took refuge in times of foreign invasion. A gate-church is exactly what it says. You enter through a large arch topped by a highly decorated church which also served as an observation post.

My heart flooded with joy as I walked slowly and reverently around the monastery grounds and visited some of its buildings. Today this Lavra is a state museum. A Lavra is a major monastery, and this title has been given to only four monasteries in Russia. The churches and other buildings are being reverently restored. I felt strongly the holiness of the place. Here, I thought, thousands of saints have lived, labored and loved. Here Nestor wrote the first Russian historical chronicals. Here millions of pilgrims wept and prayed, having traveled from all over Russia. Here the Russian Orthodox Church found its soul and had its physical center for three centuries (989 to 1299).

But most of all it was here that St. Theodosius discovered the risen Christ still suffering in his brothers

16

and sisters, a feature which attracted and influenced all Russians throughout the centuries. The great Russian writers, even those who professed to be atheists, all have stamped at the core of their spirit a predilection for the humiliati, the despised ones, the poor, the rejects, the fools. The great writers have always longed and thirsted for justice, for freedom, in the sense that all men should be free. The great writers have always opposed any kind of suppression and oppression throughout Russia's entire history up to the present—to Solzhenitsyn and Dr. Zakharov.

Theodosius loved the glorious, suffering Christ so much, he loved the serfs and the poor to such an extent, that this characteristic has been stamped upon the Russian spirit forever. Even as abbot, even as an old man, he managed to spend some time working with the serfs in the field. He helped to bring in the fire wood and the water until his very last days on earth, thus revealing to his generation the immense dignity of the poor, the dignity of "menial" work.

Tamara led us through the upper caves, a series of underground corridors and chambers where the monks spent at least part of the year in total solitude, fasting and prayer. The air, the stones, the walls exude pure holiness as you walk lightly along those narrow subterranean paths. In the early days of the monastery a great number of monks were buried there. When subsequently their caskets were opened for inspection, a strange phenomenon was observed. They had all become mummified! Today you walk by many an open casket and pray to the saint whose body is preserved there. One of the most touching scenes is the cave where "the twelve Greek brothers" lie side by side. According to tradition, they arrived at the monastery in its earliest days and with the help of a miraculous icon of Our Lady's Assumption, they built the Church of the Assump-

17

tion in a single day. They remained at the monastery, died there, and lie side by side, all twelve of them, in a little cave overlooking the broad and beautiful Dnieper River.

Because of St. Theodosius, Russian monks have always been on the side of the poor. They have, through the years, given them hospitality and work. They have nursed them back to health. They have upbraided the mighty and the wealthy, and strongly interceded with them in favor of social justice. Because of Theodosius, the Russian monk became a man of prayer, of silence, a poustinik, a staretz, a celibate available to God and man, an educator, a protector of Russian culture and a friend to every man. Most of all, he brought God to Russia. His empty heart (kenosis) opened up to God a wide channel through which he could be free to pour his mercy, his truth, his light, his love upon the peoples of this immense and mysterious land. Because of Theodosius, monasteries developed the rich and inspiring liturgy whereby men, women and children entered heaven for a few hours, were lifted up in prayer, and let their spirits soar to the very feet of God in a tremendous exchange of love. After our visit, Tamara, the Japanese professor and I just sat there on a little bench enjoying the peace and the glory of it all.

After a while we drove to Russia's first church, St. Sophia, dedicated to the Wisdom of "The God," as Tamara used to say. Not God, but "The God." First built in 1037 by St. Vladimir, it has been partly destroyed and rebuilt many times. Kiev suffered many years of occupation. In 1240 the Tartars destroyed the whole city except for some two hundred houses. Again it was conquered and occupied by the Lithuanians in 1362, by the Poles in 1569, by Moscow in 1654, by the German armies in World War I and World War II. During the last war, two hundred thousand of its people were killed or sentenced to labor camps in Germany. Nearly a hundred thousand were massacred just outside the city of Babi Yar; most of these were Jews.

St. Sophia is a glorious church, surmounted by twelve shiny cupolas. It can be seen for miles across the Dnieper. Inside, you find magnificent frescoes and mosaics dating back to the eleventh century. On the ceiling and top walls, behind the iconostasis, there is an eighteen-foot praying Virgin. Her head alone is six feet long, but because it is situated on the curve of the ceiling, the fresco is perfectly proportioned. From the floor below the Virgin, and on either side of her, you notice an unusual scene: on one side, Christ giving out Communion under the species of bread; on the other side, Christ ministering the chalice to the communicants.

Kievan Christianity reflects the human condition: the misery of man, his greed and arrogance, struggling with the mercy of God. The floor of St. Sophia's Cathedral, Russia's first church, was desecrated by its own people in the seventeenth century. The desecration remains to this day. On that floor you trod underfoot everywhere symbols of Islamism and of Judaism. A couple of centuries ago some zealots decided to show the superiority and the power of Christianity over the Muslims and the Jews. I wept in St. Sophia. My Japanese companion asked me why I was disturbed. I answered, "I am wondering how a bishop or a priest and a Christian people could possibly gather together here to offer a liturgy of forgiveness, of mercy and of love while at the same time despising our Jewish and Muslim brothers."

Together, I think we prayed quietly for the brotherhood of man under the fatherhood of God. We prayed to forgive and to be forgiven as we contemplated three generations of frescoes and icons in St. Sophia, the mother of the Russian Church, the mother of the Russian Orthodox Church.

That night at supper a sad and lonely young Ukrainian

exchanged lapel buttons with me. Russians love to give you something and also to receive what they call "a souvenir." The most popular souvenirs to bring with you, by the way, are pop records. For my gorgeous Canadian maple leaf he gave me a Polish Motor Exhibition button! The next morning as I was leaving for the Leningrad plane, the porter in the hotel exchanged my Polish Motor Exhibition button for a splendid pin of Ukrainia's greatest poet, Taras Shevchenko, who had died in 1861, after spending his whole life fighting for the poor. I was proud to wear his pin.

At the airport, the smart, intelligent, young Intourist clerk, upon meeting me, immediately touched the Shevchenko pin and then my cross. He asked in superb English, "How do you reconcile this with that?" I answered, "Christ was a poor man who died that all poor men should be cared for, that all men should become brothers. The Church is good as long as it remains poor." He was stunned. "Do you teach that to your students?" "We teach that to thousands." He was truly happy to hear that. Shevchenko wrote prophetically more than a hundred years ago:

> Justice will rise! Freedom will flow'r!
> And then to Thee alone
> All tongues will pray, all heads will bow
> For ever and for ever.
> But in the meantime, rivers flow,
> People's blood in rivers!

He had suffered much during his lifetime and had asked to be buried in Kiev.

> When I die, friend, lay my body
> Amid the spreading plain,

20

Where I would my bones were buried
In my beloved Ukraine,
That my native fields unbounded
The Dnieper and her shore
Be mine to see, as mine to hear
The raging river roar.

His body was brought from St. Petersburg and reverently laid to rest in Kiev a few weeks after his death. Today at the foot of his statue are written the closing lines of his "Testament":

And in the family of the free,
The family that will be,
Do not fail to speak a kind
And gentle word of me.

Friend, whoever you may be, may someone after we die speak gently of you, speak gently of me. Amen.

21

3. CITY OF THE INNER GLOW

Leningrad is one of the world's most beautiful cities. It has been called, with good reason, the Palmyra of the North.

Peter the Great, at the end of the seventeeth century, gave flesh to a desire which every Russian has, "To break out of his isolation and become a brother to all mankind." Peter lived for a few years in Western Europe, particularly Holland, studying construction, navigation, administration, education and the military sciences. He wanted to open Russia to the West, so he invited Western men with their ideas to a dialogue with his people.

The idea came to him to build a city from nothing, in the westernmost part of European-Russia. He set himself an impossible task—that of building a new city in the marshes and on the islands of the Neva Delta at the entrance to the Gulf of Finland. Today Leningrad rises in all its glory on a hundred and one islands connected by eight hundred bridges and crossed by hundreds of canals. It is hard to believe that much of this solid ground was marshland. Buildings had to be erected on numerous piles sunk deep into the mushy ground. The sparkling pink granite embankments cost many a workman's life, so much so that it has been said that Leningrad is built on a pile of bones.

Peter's first city, constructed in 1703, was modeled after the Amsterdam he knew, a city of canals and rather drab houses. He gave it a Dutch name, "Sankt Piter Bourkh." Within ten years foreign architects had erected thirty-five thousand buildings. Peter never was too fond of Moscow. Too many people there were opposed to many of his westernizing ideals. He moved the seat of government from Moscow to his own city. He renamed it St. Petersburg, using the German form "burg," town. In 1914 it became Petrograd, i.e., the city of Peter, in Russian, for obvious reasons. After Lenin's death it got its present name of Leningrad.

The city quickly lost its drabness, especially under Catherine the Great in the 1750s. Enormous and colorful palaces gradually replaced the original structures. The architects had a stroke of genius. Since overcast skies cover the city most of the year, they found a way of reflecting every single ray of sunshine which escaped through the clouds. They painted their buildings white with an ornate green trim, or white with a golden-yellow trim, or green with white trim, or yellow with white trim, so that the atmosphere continually glows even on a dark day.

It is impossible to exaggerate the beauty of Leningrad. Its squares, statues, parks, trees, palaces, churches easily rival and perhaps surpass the beauties of Paris and London.

I spent the last week of September there. The colorful autumn leaves still hung on the trees. The sun shone for some time everyday. People crowded the parks and Nevsky Prospect, the city's fascinating main boulevard named after St. Alexander Nevsky. He was a war hero of the thirteenth century, and the patron saint of the whole Leningrad area.

Winter, I am told, was always an especially delightful time, and still is. The canals freeze over. Thousands of people, warmly dressed, skate all over the city. For two hundred years wealthy families rode up and down the streets and canals in the most beautiful sleighs and carriages in the world, bundled in their magnificent furs from Siberia. Court life at first had been noted for its coarseness and vulgarity. Within a few years all that changed. The Winter Palace was erected, containing some five hundred rooms, each a jewel in itself. Its sumptuous ballrooms were illumined by the largest chandeliers in Europe, glittering upon marble and jade colonnades everywhere. St. Petersburg society lived in gaudy luxury. Exciting celebrations were frequent. It was common to find some five thousand of Europe's most handsome carriages and equipage standing in the great square of the Winter Palace while a major ball was going on.

Contrasting with all this wealth was the immense poverty of the working class. Leningrad (St. Petersburg) has a long history of strikes and revolutions. In 1749 the textile workers went on strike with the support of many intellectuals and many students. This tension between the nobility's luxury and the workers' misery created tremendous ferment among the city's thinking people. For some two hundred years social justice, human suffering, inequities were debated by warmhearted noblemen, by students, by the greatest geniuses of Russia. Attempts were made to correct abuses.

In December, 1825, a number of noblemen failed to bring about a more just social system. Five of them were imprisoned in the beautiful Peter and Paul Fortress, and executed. The rest were exiled to Siberia where most of them built up the cultural and educational life there. Many great men lived here in Leningrad, suffered here, and worked hard to bring about a better life for the poor. In 1917, as the whole world knows, a frigate, the Aurora, shot a blank shell at the Winter Palace. This one shot ended a way of life and ushered in the greatest revolution mankind has ever known.

It was in this atmosphere of beauty and grandeur, and of intense human suffering, during the years 1900 to 1917, that Catherine de Kolyschkine lived (later she married Baron Boris de Hueck; then Edward J. Doherty).

I lived for a few days on St. Isaac's Cathedral Square, one block from the twenty-two-room apartment where

Catherine de Kolyschkine learned from God and her parents to love and serve the suffering Christ in every person. She grew up in a loving family, well-trained by her father and mother who fostered in her an immense hunger for knowledge and beauty and love.

The 1917 revolution did not catch her unprepared. She saw in it the hand of God calling his people to repentance. The rich had sinned. Now by God's mercy they were given the opportunity to atone. She lost everything. Physical hunger became her constant companion. She scavenged through the trash cans of back alleyways looking for potato peelings or bones or any scrap of food. She experienced nightly the terror of hobnailed boots stomping in the dark hours along the corridors of her apartment house, soldiers of the Red Army coming to arrest someone to face a firing squad or be exiled to a concentration camp.

Daily I walked by her apartment house and pondered the events which had shaped her destiny. I saw her in winter, being driven by a splendid, liveried coachman down Nevsky Boulevard, where young men in other sleighs raced and showed off for the benefit of a beautiful blonde girl. I saw her visiting the splendid shops on the same street, especially the Brentano bookstore. I heard her playing the piano, laughing, glowing at dress-up parties in her home's ballroom.

She grew up in an atmosphere of freedom, for children were beloved in St. Petersburg. They could walk down any street; they were respected by strangers. Policemen directed them back home with endearing terms. I saw her running as a little girl to St. Isaac's Cathedral two blocks away and marveling at the gorgeous, baroque Russian-Italian-French architecture, frescoes and icons. I saw a little girl become suddenly quiet and silent, drawn to the altar and to the dove above the altar where God lives among men in a very powerful way. I saw a young woman's heart opening itself to that power, that mercy, that peace, that joy, that love.

In that very church she witnessed in horror some Red Army soldiers kill an old priest and trample the Eucharist underfoot, while an old man prayed, "Father forgive them *even though they know* what they do." At that moment of great loss she realized forever the immense value of the priesthood.

I loved Leningrad, its fascinating streets, its beautiful canals, its gorgeous palaces, but most of all, *its inner glow.* Perhaps I felt there a little of what Catherine Doherty had experienced in depth. . .the presence of God. Just as the sun rarely shines in full splendor here, so God rarely manifests himself in his full glory. I felt him pulsating at the heart of this city which has bred so many seekers after the absolute: revolutionaries, great writers, saints. God doesn't allow for mediocrity here. He prods, he calls, he glows.

Walking all over the Winter Palace Square and down many streets, I prayed that Leningrad might always experience unrest, ferment, and hunger for God, for the absolute, for peace and for justice.

Sunday morning I woke up early, filled with an eager desire to pray, to pilgrim, to offer the Divine Liturgy at the Leningrad Theological Seminary. I had heard that the seminary was somewhere on the grounds of the old Nevsky Lavra (a monastery built by Peter the Great). So I walked the five kilometers from the golden-spired Admiralty Building, down Nevsky Prospect to the Monastery.

It was early. Few people were on the streets. I passed by the single-cupolaed, colonnaded Cathedral of Our Lady of Kazan, one of Leningrad's most precious churches, now called "The Museum of the History of Religion and Atheism." On a previous day I had visited this notorious museum. Expecting to meet the devil face to face (!) I had first exorcised the place and sprinkled some holy water.

The museum disappointed me—it is so adolescent. It portrays in a very poor way things I had learned before making my First Communion—that some priests do not always live up to their ideals, some drink too much, some have mistresses, some abuse their power, and some are avaricious. "Dear Atheists, excuse me if I laughed at all this inanity!" To my great delight I found an icon corner and felt that gradually Russian good sense would prevail. Gradually they would remove from this glorious temple its gross, naive pictures, and restore it to its original purpose. The real name of the museum at this time should be "The History of the Sins of Some Clergymen."

This bright sunny morning my heart was light and gay as I passed by Our Lady of Kazan Cathedral and quietly blessed the people sitting in the park in front. I kept walking, praying the Rosary of Our Lady, adoring the glorious Christ in each person I met, saying, "Jesus, mercy," for myself and all mankind.

I passed by numerous bookstores, butcher shops, grocery stores, clothing stores, cafes, restaurants. I crossed many a little bridge and glanced down many a beautiful canal. Nevsky Prospect ends at the old road leading to Moscow, some five hundred miles away. I continued walking straight ahead, down a little street which led to a walled enclosure. I entered through a wide arch and discovered a graveyard to the right and to the left. A few yards away stood an old, battered church surrounded by old, battered, red-brick buildings. The Divine Liturgy was being celebrated in the church, but something inside of me said, "Go to the seminary."

I left the church and knocked at many doors in vain. Later I found out that the monastery buildings had been used as a factory since the revolution. It was Sunday. Everything was locked up tight. Urged on by some strange power I walked clear across a huge park. Families were gathering for a picnic. I came to a little muddy path skirting a canal, but with no seminary in sight anywhere. Finally I said to God, "Don't you think that I have pilgrimed and prayed enough? I'd appreciate finding the seminary right *now*. Amen."

I turned a corner. An old red-brick building beckoned. The door was open. Inside a lady sat behind a wicket. I know very little Russian but managed to convey the fact that I was a Canadian tourist anxious to visit the seminary. Immediately a young man dressed in a black suit with Roman collar came from behind the partition, took me by the hand and in hand. We went upstairs, down a long corridor, turned into a dark, tiny space and climbed a circular staircase which led directly into the sanctuary—behind the iconostasis—of the seminary chapel. The young man signaled me to a little stool by the wall. A bishop was just beginning the Divine Liturgy, accompanied by two other bishops and fifteen priests, all standing around the altar and dressed in splendid gold vestments. Two hundred and eight seminarians sang with love, reverence and excellence the various responses. The chapel was packed with lay people.

My heart was suffused with a tremendous peace and joy as I sat there—the stranger, the foreigner, the beggar, the poor man, the pilgrim admitted to the heavenly feast. The main celebrant prayed like Jesus ascending the hill of Golgotha. His face furrowed with sorrow, his whole being praised and wept and interceded.

During the homily a priest came to me. He spoke some English. I entrusted to his care the love and prayers of Catherine Doherty, of the Madonna House Apostolate, and of the thousands of people who were accompanying me on this pilgrimage. His eyes shone with joy. I told him I was a Roman Catholic priest. I made bold to ask him if I could concelebrate at this Orthodox liturgy. Reluctantly he answered, "I cannot give you this permission but the Metropolitan can." I said, "Metropolitan Nikodim, the Archbishop of Leningrad and Novgorod?" He said, "The same."

This was indeed an unexpected gift from God. For years I had read about the holy Metropolitan, of his great love for the Orthodox Church, and of his untiring efforts in the field of ecumenism...Truly a luminary of the Christian Church today! Although only forty-five, he had been a bishop many years and had already suffered three serious heart attacks due to the unbelievable pressures of his office. I had long admired and loved him. What a kindness on God's part to allow me this privilege.

The Metropolitan very graciously acceded to my request. I was given proper vestments and took my place among my Orthodox brothers. At the kiss of peace, the Archbishop addressed me in Latin as he gave me the kiss of Christ. At communion time he again graciously used the Roman formulae when he gave the Lord's body and blood. After communion, a current of happiness passed through all our hearts. Everyone of the priests came to greet me. Some offered me a little break-of-the-fast of hot wine and bread.

Metropolitan Nikodim sat down and called me over. He had a most precious gift for me—the remnants of the holy bread which had not been used in the liturgy, to bring back to Canada and to a lady from Leningrad. "I shall always remember this liturgy," I whispered. He answered immediately, "Remember only one thing, 'Pray for me.'" I was happy to tell him of the many, many people who were doing just that. He smiled and kissed me three times. Truly I was received as a brother by all the priests and as a friend by the great archbishop.

After the liturgy I met Orthodox seminarians from many parts of the world, a very friendly Japanese

Orthodox priest, and I visited my friend Dostoyevsky's grave on the way out. That evening an American specialist on Dostoyevsky, and his wife, had dinner with me.

At night I thanked God for having led me all through the day and lavished upon me such precious and unforgettable gifts, moments, privileges, graces and memories. I had manipulated nothing. I had determined nothing. I had organized nothing, but simply tried to listen to God and let him have his way with me. Perhaps the greatest lesson I learned in Russia was just that, "to abandon myself to God, let him have his way, and follow, follow, follow..." even down a tiny, mucky path, which had led me to glory that morning in Leningrad.

4. THE SLUMBER OF THE GREAT LORD NOVGOROD

Intourist drove me in a private taxi down Nevsky Boulevard, thick with crowds, to the big and beautiful Moscow railroad station. I was bidding a reluctant goodbye to Leningrad, the City of the Inner Glow. It was early at night and I was about to take the train for the ancient and revered city of *Novgorod*, three hours away.

A young man from Intourist opened the taxi door and greeted me with a gentle smile as we pulled up to the curb. He had a porter take my luggage to my coach seat. I wanted a sandwich for the journey and especially something to drink: mineral water or preferably a Russian fruit drink, which is quite good. It is officially called "Limonad," mildly carbonated, and made from apples, oranges, lemons or some other fruits. We searched in vain with only fifteen minutes left before departure. The affable young man led me to my seat on the train. Ten minutes later he returned with two huge sesame-seed buns and a fruit drink. Delightedly he proffered his gifts, refusing any monetary compensation. "It has been a great joy for me to speak with you," he gently said.

The trains of the Soviet Union ride smoothly. They pull out without jerking and stop without throwing you out of your seat.

I find peaceful trains conducive to praying, dreaming, reminiscing. They provide an organic transition from one experience to another, an opportunity to assimilate the last few days' high points of delight and discovery, and integrate them into my inner being forever. Leningrad took root in my spirit during this ride. It enriched me with its treasures. It carved out for itself a room in my heart

31

and filled it with graceful buildings, quiet canals and a ravishing glow.

Slowly, that room filled with many people: Metropolitan Nikodim entered with his priests and seminarians, the courteous chambermaids at the hotel, a lady who laughed at my shouting "Rasputin," busy Intoursit clerks, Swedish businessmen with whom I had had so much fun one night at supper, a delightful and distinguished American couple, the sultry singer who had belted out "Now I'm a Believer" that first night in the restaurant, the mixed road crew of men and women repairing a piece of the Winter Palace Square one sunny afternoon.

Faces passed before my eyes, the thousands of faces who had revealed to me the Suffering Christ, on the streets or packed in trolley cars, queueing up at every stall, every counter, every store.

My heart filled with the thousands of lay people, priests, monks, bishops who had been tortured and imprisoned since 1917 on an island in Lake Ladoga, close by Leningrad. I cried out for all men who still suffer from repression or imprisonment. They are our most precious members, the Christ among us crucified over and over again for each generation. I remembered the two hundred thousand persons who had died of starvation in World War II during nine hundred bloody days of siege and blockade. I "saw" a light shining, a warmth and comfort emanating from Catherine Doherty's apartment, covering all the misery with a mantle of tenderness.

The full moon was out as we sped comfortably through the night, its light revealing thousands of thin, twisted trees standing like so many suffering wraiths, and consoling each one.

It was half-past ten when we arrived in the ancient City, the Republic of Novgorod, so admired by historians for its love of freedom and independence that it was personalized and named "His Majesty, the Great Lord Novgorod."

Russian blood contains many strong strains. The Slav tribes that came down to Kiev and to the Novgorod area in the seventh and eight centuries had already been greatly enriched by their environment. The Caucasus is still one of the healthiest regions in the world; old age there means anything above a hundred years. Many had come from the wild Carpathian mountains carrying rich beliefs, myths and traditions in their spirit. Novgorod stands on the banks of the Volkhov River, midway between the Baltic Sea and Kiev. It was soon to be conquered and ruled by another strong, healthy, mystical people, the Vikings, whom Russians called Varangians (and also Normans).

I had always thought that Russia was "East" and we were "West". . ."and never the twain could meet." It was quite a surprise to discover that the East-West conflict began from the first day of Russia's history and is deeply rooted in the Russian soul. Indeed, official Russian history begins in Novgorod in 862 when Rurik and his men: Vikings, Swedes, Westerners, Varangians, were invited to the area and then conquered it and built there the "New City," the New Gorod. The Slavs, Swedes, Germans, Lithuanians and Tatars married and intermarried over the centuries to form a very distinctive people whose inner strength is so rich that is can absorb and assimilate, digest or reject any culture without fear of losing its own identity.

These various strains, and especially the East-West conflict at the very heart of the nation, have become a tremendous creative force, an energizing tension, an enriching struggle. Who does not know that Russia's artistic achievements stand out as works of genius? Think of its literature, ballet, iconography, frescoes, music, architecture. Think of its monasteries, its saints, its hunger for God, its struggle with God, its deep insights into the mystery of God, of pain and of joy, and you will have a sense of its greatness and its mystery.

I arrived at the Sadko hotel on the outskirts of the city now numbering some 160,000 inhabitants. Sadko, I was told, is a legendary hero noted for his keen mind, his wit and his marital fidelity. Captured by the sea god, he won his freedom by charming his captor with music, with dances and with poetry. In turn, the god offered him the most beautiful maidens of the kingdom for his concubine, but Sadko remained faithful to his wife. Impressed by such loyalty and charmed by his wit, the god let him go free. Sadko returned home to Novgorod to live happily ever after with his loving wife and family.

The sun was shining the next morning as I began walking in the footsteps of the great people who had lived here since 862. My guide first took me to the trade side of the Volkhov River. Novgorod soon grew rich and prospered after its foundation by Rurik. His son, Oleg, captured Kiev, and for some three hundred years a son of the Kievan prince ruled Novgorod. But its people chafed under any kind of autocracy. By the twelfth century an interesting system of government had been developed, made up of the best elements of monarchy, oligarchy and democracy. The prince was hired by contract, and his powers and duties were strictly outlined. He was mostly a military leader, a protector of the city from its enemies.

Its most famous prince was St. Alexander Nevsky. Alexander lived in Suzdal, some four hundred miles northeast of Novgorod. He was only twenty-one when the Novgorodians invited him to be their prince, their military leader. In July, 1240, he crushed the Catholic Swedes on the River Neva from which his name was derived as a title of honor and a remembrance of his conquest. In 1242, he repulsed the Teutonic Knights who had come to "christianize" the area. In 1246 he repelled the pagan Lithuanians. Realizing that he could not conquer the Mongols, he made a treaty with them. Novgorod would remain free from the Mongol terror by paying a tribute to Batu Kahn, the great chief.

From 1136 to 1478—when it was conquered by Moscow—the city was ruled mostly by the *Veche* or public assembly in which all citizens participated but which was mostly influenced by the merchant oligarchy. Those were the great days of Novgorod. Its people prospered. Beautiful buildings were erected in abundance. Schools of painting, iconography and architecture developed. Its glory was known from the Northern Sea to Constantinople, from Constantinople to Persia.

Facing the trade area on the other side of the river was the fortress, known in every other city as the kremlin, but not in Novgorod. True to their independent spirit they called their fortress the Citadel. Although the center of military protection, the Citadel's main glory has always been the majestic Church of St. Sophia, first built in 1045 by Vladimir II, son of Yaroslav the Wise, Prince of Kiev. St. Sophia shines all white in the sun with no exterior decorations save the one fresco topping the entrance. Inside, large frescoes are being restored. It is a huge building. The upstairs gallery leads to a number of rooms now used to display old manuscripts, books, religious antiques, etc.

East and West have always clashed in Novgorod. The trade embankment was known for its Western leanings. The St. Sophia and Citadel side stood for pure Slavic culture and eventually for union with Moscow. Moscow has always been the center of pure Slavic culture.

My guides generally began their contact with me in a rather curt and formal manner, but as we toured and as I listened carefully to their words it seemed to me that the Suffering Christ in them and the Suffering Christ in me became one. A bond and a peace gradually did form, or so it seemed to me. At any rate, within an hour or so, invariably each one began to relax and went out of his way to show me things they guessed would be of special interest to a priest. They always amazed me, for I expected no special treatment and certainly asked for none. As a matter of fact, I had determined upon arriving in Russia that I would not even ask any questions of anyone but would simply accept and receive whatever they wished to tell me.

My guide in Novgorod finished the tour at the Citadel by introducing me to a very great man who also happens to be a very great restorer of paintings. He has been hired by the government to put together four hundred thousand fresco pieces from the Church of the Transfiguration of Our Lord, situated some four kilometers from the city center and which had been blown up in World War II. Imagine the immense task involved in separating all the pieces that make up one fresco from four hundred thousand chunks of plaster.

How graciously he received me! The joy with which he shared his treasures with me remains one of the high points of my encounter with the Russian soul. "It is ennobling to touch the fourteenth century," he said. Many students spend their holidays working with him, assiduously, laboriously, painstakingly seeking pieces that fit fragments to add to one fresco or to begin another.

The best religious art: icons, frescoes, churches, was done between the eleventh and the sixteenth centuries. It was done with extreme care and with great love. That's why "It is ennobling to touch the fourteenth century." Pray for this great man and his work which ennobles all of us. When he has a fresco partly together he paints an exact copy of it, revealing an unusual humility for an artist: a total submission to the original artist. I commented on the exactness of his copies. He replied, "It is because I love the originals."

Following this extraordinary, unexpected discovery, he highly recommended that I should visit another Church of the Transfiguration of Our Lord, also dating from the fourteenth century, still intact, being restored, and situated on the trade side of Novgorod. The attractions there are the frescoes of Theophanes the Greek. We embraced a la Russe and parted.

At one time every street and every block in every street of the trade area had its own church. Some of them were open to the general public; many were used simply as private chapels for a rich merchant's family and relatives. A number of these churches still exist, separated from each other only by a few hundred feet—the Church of St. Nicholas, the Church of the Myrrh-Bearing Women, the Church of the Dormition of Our Lady, of St. George, of St. Procopius. I noticed some Celtic crosses on one eleventh-century church.

The Church of St. Paraskeva interested me particularly—not so much the church as St. Paraskeva herself. Her name in Greek means "Friday"; she had a great devotion to the passion of Our Lord Jesus Christ. The merchants adopted her as their patron saint. Do you know why? Because Friday was the big market day. "Friday" in Russian is *Piatnitza*, so she is known officially as St. Paraskeva-Piatnitza. She was born in Iconia, Asia Minor, and martyred during the persecution of Diocletian in the fourth century. Her feast is celebrated on October 28th. She is also the patroness of women's work. Her icon represents her standing, holding the cross of martyrdom in her right hand, the scroll of the creed unrolled in her left hand, indicating she was a bold preacher of the gospel. On her head, the white cloth of virginity is topped by a patrician diadem.

Paraskeva through the years became one of Orthodoxy's very famous saints. I grew quite fond of her while walking

37

around the grounds blessed by her invisible presence for so many centuries. A short distance away stands a very attractive little church bearing some delightful exterior decorations. Its special charm to me lay in the fact that the exterior symbols *were not symmetrical.* One side didn't balance the other geometrically, and yet the whole effect was quite pleasant. It made me realize once again that life is not mathematical nor even logical.

As I stood wondering at this strange beauty, I thought of the great struggle in which the people of the Soviet Union are engaged at the present time, just as we are in the Western world: the struggle to unite technology and life, mathematics and reality, abstract intellect and the warmth of a living, creative spirit, animus and anima, action and contemplation, the inveterate masculine and the eternal feminine. I sensed deeply that the anima, the feminine, is the great hope of our whole world. Men must stop raping the earth, polluting its purity, killing its life. All of us, men and women, need to care more, to love more, to reverence this beautiful creation entrusted to us by a loving God. Women, the feminine, are the hope of all mankind as well as of the Soviet Union.

The previous evening, at supper, a Red Army officer and his wife sat in front of me. He was cold, precise, dry as an old stick. She was bouncy, warm, happy, completely beyond him and caring for him most tenderly, a healthy woman, beautiful, breasty, earthy, totally free of any slavery to mathematics or technology or intellect—alive and life-giving.

The next morning I had breakfast in the buffet. Each hotel has at least one restaurant and two or three buffets where you can get food and drink, especially when the restaurant is closed. Three women dentists from Leningrad, here for a dental convention, breakfasted with me. They too were alive, full of humor, generous. They insisted on sharing some delicious meat with me. Not only the Soviet Union but the whole world needs men and women who care.

The lady guardian at the Church of the Transfiguration signaled to me. She snapped me out of my reverie. She indicated that I had better go in now because the church would soon be locked for the night. I went in eagerly to admire the frescoes of Theophanes the Greek, the greatest religious painter of Russia, second only to the incomparable master of them all, Andrei Rublev, of whom we shall speak more later on.

Theophanes fascinated me. Here was a Greek from Constantinople accustomed to logic, trained in mathematics and in the rather severe type of Byzantine iconography. He arrived in Novgorod in the fourteenth century at the age of forty and within weeks he had become Russian to the core. I found that most extraordinary. What a beauty he discovered in the Russian spirit. What a love must have been in his heart to uncover that beauty so quickly, so deeply as to become one of its finest exponents. The tear of God with which each Russian soul is scalded, the pain of Christ, the pain of all mankind stare at you from his frescoes. The triumph of the risen Christ shines powerfully through that immense suffering.

I left Novgorod with the Paschal mystery more deeply formed in my heart, ever more convinced that glory and freedom are born from the pain of man united with the pain of Christ, ever more amazed at the dignity and the glory of man, at the radiant tenderness and glory of God. His Majesty, the Great Lord Novgorod slumbers now. The city has lost touch with its past greatness. I am convinced it will live again and arise to new heights of freedom and glory soon.

5. FIRE IN THE FROZEN CITY

The Moscow train left Novgorod at night. I awoke early enough to greet the dawn rising on the horizon. The railroad entrance to Moscow is like that of most major cities: shacks, drab apartment houses, factories.

All through the day my spirit was oppressed by some vague but powerful sadness. It made me pray all the more. This despondency surprised me because my previous days had been truly happy ones.

Like every megapolis, Moscow can neither be defined nor embraced. It beggars description as does Tokyo, Paris, New York or London. How often have you not heard a visitor to one of these phenomenal cities struggle to express his impressions. For instance, people will say: "To me, Paris is les Champs Elysees, la Place de l'Etoile, le Louvre"; "to me, Paris is a Notre-Dame and le Sacré-Coeur"; "to me, Paris is students rioting in the daytime and cavorting in the nighttime"; "to me, Paris is a small, cold, inconvenient hotel where the lift never works"; "to me, Paris is the banks of the Seine with its bookstalls and sidewalk painters"; "to me, Paris is nostalgia, the Merry Widow, Maxim's and the great Bernhardt." I wonder what *Parisians* say about Paris? In the working-class district—the "Red Belt" around the city of Light—I met a family years ago who said, "To us, Paris is Hell."

You've been there—to London, to New York, to Rome, to Chicago. Can you describe any of these fascinating human achievements and conglomerations?

Just as London is not England, and New York is not the United States of America, so Moscow is not the Soviet Union. What is Moscow? A huge city which reminded me

40

more of New York or London than of Russia. Had it not been for the language, on my first day there I would have thought I had landed in New York with an added touch of Chicago! The hectic pace, the rat race, the heavy traffic, the rushing crowds, the nervous and intense clerks: they were all there. Large cities sap the psychic energies of their inhabitants except, of course, Rome, where people may rush but less frantically. Romans have a greater love for living than for getting anywhere. (My favorite city is Lisbon where the word "rat race" does not exist, where "rushing" still has to be invented.)

Moscow rushes like New York, perhaps more. Tourist personnel there had much in common with the curt, cold, abrasive tourist personnel I had met in Paris. I found it as dull as a London pub at three o'clock of a wet afternoon.

I was told that Moscow has everything: the best ballet in the world, and that is true; GUM, the largest store in the country and perhaps, in the whole world, also true. Special deluxe restaurants offer "National" cuisine at "supernational" prices. (Strange how difficult it is to get Russian food in Moscow!) Theaters, cinemas abound. Two theaters are required now to accomodate the fans of the ever-popular Circus. The ballet is so good that most perform-ances of the Bolshoi Company are held in the Kremlin's Palace of Congresses which seats six thousand people, rather than in the Bolshoi's own theater which seats only two thousand.

As everyone knows, Moscow is the seat of government, the seat of power of the Union of the Soviet Socialist Republics. From the Kremlin, two hundred sixty million people are governed: plans are concocted for the growth and development of one-sixth of the earth's surface; and deals are made with most of the world's countries.

Trucks by the thousands thunder by on every street, threatening your sanity, and your life should you attempt to cross at an intersection.

Yes, Moscow has everything except a smile, except spontaneity, except imagination, except spirit. As people flock in—the population is now close to eight million—grey rectangular apartment blocks shoot up to desecrate their lives and the landscape.

"Moscow, O Moscow, city of the walking dead where nobody laughs and nobody cries, what terrible crimes have been committed in you to make you so pallid, so faceless, so deadening to the human spirit. Were Malikovsky—who loved you so much—living today, would he still say, 'I would choose to live and die in Paris if there were not a city like Moscow'? I don't think so. He would run from you both."

What can a heart do here, a pilgrim's heart, a sinner's heart? Weep copious tears, for my own sins, for our crimes, for the sins of all mankind. "I can see how Violence and Discord fill the city; day and night they stalk together along the city walls. Sorrow and Misery live inside, ruin is an inmate; Tyranny and Treachery are never absent from its central square" (Psalm 54).

In my small hotel room I offered Mass immediately upon arrival. After breakfast in the restaurant overlooking Red Square and the Kremlin, I hurried on foot to the Tretiakov Gallery, a State Museum, where Holy Russia's two most precious and venerated icons are exhibited: the *Trinity* of Andrei Rublev and *Our Lady of Vladimir*. How much I longed to pray in front of these two icons, before which thousands of saints had prayed. I felt that the special presence of God in them would wash me clean of evil and bring peace to my beleaguered spirit. Something in the atmosphere was oppressing me to death and I hurried to Our Lady and to the Trinity for relief.

On my way to the Tretiakov Museum I crossed the Moscow River. Halfway over the bridge I turned back to

42

contemplate a glorious scene: the Kremlin stood there with its red-pink walls, its fifteen and more towers, the white and gold Palace of the Tzars—now the seat of the Supreme Soviet and of the House of Nationalities. The Kremlin churches with their gold and blue cupolas rose up to the sky like so many tongues of fire surmounted by a cross reaching out to meet the cross and the fire coming down from heaven. I wanted to be photographed with that background. A young man was leaning against the bridge's granite parapet. I asked him to take my picture. He responded at once. He had seemed rather listless and bored. Perhaps I was the answer to his boredom.

He insisted on accompanying me to the Museum. I explained to him that I was going there to pray. That didn't bother him. A non-practicing Muslim from Samarkand in the south, he told me he was leaving for home the next day. He showed me his ticket. He liked me.

We walked quickly through a multitude of rooms, hardly noticing what they contained. All of a sudden I found myself directly in front of Rublev's masterpiece, the *Old Testament Trinity*.

I had often read and spoken of God's love, of the incredible life of love which unites Father, Son and Holy Spirit. I had often seen reproductions of this famous icon. But I had never seen Love so clearly painted before my very eyes. That's what I saw immediately, without effort, without analysis: Love. I stood transfixed, unaware of the crowds milling by, caught up in the greatest reality that is. I saw with my own eyes how much the Father loves the Son and the Holy Spirit, how much the Son loves his Father and the Spirit, how much the Spirit loves the Father and the Son. It was an incredible, unforgettable experience, totally unexpected.

I had come there crying out, "Lord, have mercy; Lord, have mercy; Lord, have mercy," my heart filled with unbearable anguish. I had come to prostrate myself before the all-holy One, to implore his forgiveness, to repeat forty

43

times and four hundred times "Lord, have mercy." But I was greeted with the vision of overwhelming love which literally took my breath away. God revealed to me a bit of his glory at that moment. He seemed to say: "Moscow and you and all mankind and everything that exists has its origin and its home within my all-embracing Love. Indeed, I am merciful and loving. Evil is as nothing in the face of my Love and crumbles into dust at my slightest touch."

I stood there for a long time, relieved beyond measure of the heavy burden I had brought to the Trinity, and I praised God for his love, for his mercy, for his great glory. I praised him *for being Love* and for having made us out of love to love and be loved. I marveled at the gentleness of each Person gazing upon the Others. I was astounded by the infinite humility of each Person. I knew "that all was well and that all manner of things would be well," irrespective of our sinfulness and stupidity.

Then I moved to the next room, also full of icons, to be greeted at the far end by the celebrated and oldest icon of Russia, *Our Lady of Vladimir.* It is a twelfth-century gift from Constantinople. For many years it was venerated in a special church of the ancient city of Vladimir—whence its name—and was brought to Moscow in the fifteenth century. Since the revolution it was taken from its church in Moscow and transferred to the Tretiakov Gallery, a State Museum, where thousands come to meet Our Lady weekly, people from all over Russia and tourists from all over the world.

As I have mentioned before, this is an icon of tenderness. You cannot help but be moved by the tender bonds uniting Mother and Child and drawing you into that holy and loving circle. Mary, the Mother of God, continues to watch over her beloved people. Anyone who looks at her cannot help but know that he is loved.

The curators of the Museum have treated Our Lady of

Vladimir with reverence. Her icon stands on a pedestal, encased in glass, with nothing hung on the wall behind her to distract one's attention. All you see is her, the Bogomater, and her little Son, Jesus, the Lord. For more than eight hundred years people have prayed before this glorious image. People have wept. People have found hope. I did too. I left the Tretiakov Gallery with spirits renewed and heart aflame with love, with joy, with hope.

I should say *we* left! My friend had been standing quietly at a distance. He insisted on treating me to a light lunch and walking me back to my hotel. I gradually realized that he wanted to spend the day and night in my room and in my bed! He insisted on knowing my room number. I gave him the wrong one. I thanked him profusely for his kindness and gentleness and I walked away. I showered, and slept for a couple of hours. God had given me so much spiritual joy that day. I wished I could have passed it on to this fine young Muslim.

It was ten o'clock in the evening by the time I finished writing my letters and diary. I was hungry. Although the restaurant doesn't close before eleven, four waiters were standing in line at its door, shouting with gusto, in chorus, like a barbershop quartet, one of the Russians' absolutely favorite words, "Zacrito," which means "closed." How the clerks in a store, the cashiers of the bank, the girls at an Intourist desk, love to say "Zacrito, Zacrito, Zacrito," and once more with a louder voice "Zacrito." It produces in them a major catharsis. All the frustrations and problems of the day slough off their shoulders. Their eyes shine and their cheeks glow.

The soul-satisfying effect of "Zacrito" is topped only by "Nyet Nyet," "No, No." It has to be vigorously emitted at least twice, better three times, or, supreme beatitude, four times. I quickly discovered that any waiter or waitress automatically and with assurance immediately responded to my first choice from the menu with resounding "Nyets."

Why not make them happy, I thought. From there on I carefully picked out from the menu as my first choices a couple of items I didn't want and which I guessed might not be easily available. My waiters went into orgies of "Nyets," a cathartic experience beyond their wildest expectations. After that I could order the moon on a silver platter. The service became rapid, gracious, impeccable.

Another thing which makes any member of the Russian personnel happy is the opportunity of saying "Come back in an hour," "Come back tomorrow," "Come back next week." "Come back next year" throws them into total delirium. Watch that. One of my clerks didn't show up for a week afterwards.

But all this is an aside. I was hungry, and the restaurant wouldn't let me in. Knowing that all restaurants close around eleven I ran out of the hotel in search of food, not having eaten since noon, and then only a small open-faced sandwich, "Butterbrod," the only kind available in any of the Soviet Union's eight million square miles.

Across the street, an upstairs eating-place beckoned. I reached it through an underground passage, illumined, decorated, crowded. The head-waitress seated me—reluctantly, for it was near closing time—at a table with two men, under forty, affable, married. They were drinking some green thing with a yellow spot at its center, barely discernible in the dim lights. The menu listed only drinks and ice cream. (All you American citizens stand up and cheer. You have won the cold war, hands down!) Would you believe that the most popular dessert in the U.S.S.R. is ice cream?—good ice cream, better than any of Howard Johnson's twenty-eight varieties, I kid you not. It comes all decorated, two scoops, one on top of the other, shaped like onion domes, with a dab of fruit, syrup, meringue.

I ordered ice cream and the same kind of drink which my two companions highly recommended. That drink turned out to be utterly delicious. The yellow spot was a raw egg, just what I needed. I shared another drink with them, this time without the egg. We communicated easily. They lived an hour away. It was getting late and tomorrow was Monday and back to work. They asked me about myself. "I'm a priest." "A priest!" They pointed to girls, "Do you have one of those?" "Nyet," I answered. "Nyet!" they said, "how can you live?"

"It's not that hard. There are many other joys in my life, especially the freedom to love everybody, women as well as men, and all things. It's not that easy either. Pray for me."

"Pray? What's that?"

"Talk to Bogo (God), to Bogomater (Mary)."

I gave them a medal of Our Lady of Combermere for themselves and for their wives. They were delighted. They smiled from ear to ear.

This kind of thing happened to me several times in Russia. The surprise and amazement at the possibility of continency was a joy to behold. Something primordial, atavistic stirred in their depths. Beautiful memories were awakened of saints and monks and another era which had honored virginity. Communists, atheists gave me the impression that they felt a share in my kind of life. We are all responsible for every sin, we are all healed by every goodness. Jesus, the virgin-man, loves and virginizes every man and every woman. Jesus, the moderate drinker, moderates every drunk. Jesus, the humble man, fritters away our arrogance. Jesus, the gentle one, liquidates our anger. We may hate and kill; we may pretend and hide our real motives; we may lust for pleasure, profit and power. Relax. We are licked. Love dogs our heels. Love knows our name. Love calls our bluff.

47

Free as we may be, we have no chance. Our heart's hunger always betrays us, and delivers us, helpless, into the Enemy's hands. We are ravished by love. "Blessed, immense Love, what else but you is worth the gamble of our lives? You, most Dear of all dear ones, you most Precious of all precious ones, you, best Beloved among all the beloved. In Thee all are beloved. I love you."

A priest belongs to all men. Each person can lay claim upon him. He dare not indulge himself for fear of weakening his gift of peace, of hope, of healing. He dare not stop loving, lest "thousands of his brothers and sisters die from the cold."

Because he yearns and hungers for fulfillment as much, if not more, than anyone else, you, dear one, can confess any crime to him without fear of being condemned. You are understood and forgiven. In the experience of his own sinfulness and forgiveness the priest has been fashioned by the Holy Spirit into a receptacle for your anguish. Your loneliness finds a home in his heart. Jesus the Lord, the Innocent One, receives you there and heals your wounds with his tender compassion. Difficult as continency might be, it forms the priest into a father. He comes to experience an immense joy through an immense pain.

Celibacy, (virginity, continency, chastity) produces many good effects. The human race as a whole has always reverenced the virgin, the celibate dedicated to love. In the Soviet Union every single person who discovered I was a celibate reacted with surprise and some kind of strange joy. Many of them were avowed atheists yet they were pleased.

Chastity disciplines, softens the heart and lessens arrogance. It makes one compassionate and receptive to the pain of another. The warm and passionate celibate— whether man or woman—becomes in his very person a bond of union among his brothers and sisters. It has always seemed to me that celibacy's greatest effect was to help unite men and women into the one family of God. True, there is a contradiction here and also a suffering. One refuses to indulge in sexual union, holy and beautiful though it may be. Out of this abstention, like an immense force, comes forth an incredible power to unite hearts with each other, to elevate and reconcile the human spirit with God, all-embracing Love.

Yes, it amazed and rejoiced me to see with my own eyes that communists and atheists want "their" priests to be generous, to be sober, to be self-sacrificing. You can have some wine in moderation, but they don't like to see you guzzling vodka. They want a priest to live out who he is.

And I want Russians to live out who they are. Like the Jews, they too are a chosen people, mysteriously but assuredly touched by God. There may be many reasons for the traditional antagonism between Jew and Russian. They are both a chosen people. Unconsciously they compete with each other for some kind of stupid supremacy. Vaguely they both feel the guilt of not always being who they are. Their love is needed by all of us, and their loyaltv to God. The wisdom he has revealed to them is mankind's common property.

"Father, Father, let all the bells of Moscow ring out again, all of them. When Moscow numbered a hundred thousand people, it boasted of sixteen hundred bells. How many are there today? Father, let them all ring out. Let them ring without ceasing. Let them awaken the joy, the love you have hidden in those eight million hearts. Let their glorious peals soften all hearts including the Soviet rulers' hearts. Let their sound reach out all over the world breaching divisions, filling the empty spaces among men, thrilling every heart. Father, you chose the Russian people and their bells to bring us your joy. Today we miss them. We need them. Hear our prayer and let the bells of

Moscow ring out in every heart soon. We ask you this through the loving intercession of Our Lady of Vladimir. Father, Yahweh, Allah, Jesus, we dry up unless the Jew and the Russian love you. We die if they refuse us their love. Moscow and Tel-Aviv are half dead today though each one stands before the fountain of your living waters. These holy cities are being poisoned by fear and lust for power. Father, we implore you, turn them away from the bitter water holes and gently bend their heads to sip of your peace and love. The whole world will revive."

6. ROMANCE IN VLADIMIR

The train for Vladimir was not leaving until five p.m. This gave me ample time to visit the great Kremlin churches. They stand together in a sort of square, and were built before 1550. There is the Church of the Archangel Michael—Russia's special protector—where many czars and princes are buried, and the Church of the Annunciation, which contains the world's oldest extant Iconostasis, painted by Andrei Rublev around 1420. I was surprised to discover that the Russians invented the iconostasis, which became popularized later on all over the Orthodox world. Rublev's iconostasis, separating the altar from the nave, consists of rows of icons rising from the floor to the ceiling.

The Church of the Twelve Apostles and the adjoining palace became the Metropolitan's home when he moved from Vladimir to Moscow in 1326. I decided to visit the Church of the Dormition of Our Lady (Assumption) at a future date. These gorgeous temples all wear brilliant, shiny, golden and blue cupolas. Following the classical tradition, the exteriors are white and without decoration. Ivan the Terrible and his children are buried behind the iconostasis of St. Michael's Cathedral. Ivan, who ruled Russia as an autocrat during the first half of the sixteenth century, has been called "terrible" for two reasons. First, because he was cruel. Second, because he was awesome. A military and political genius, he united much of present-day Russia and gave it stability. His son Dmitri, allegedly murdered by Boris Godunov, is buried under a special baldaquin in front of the iconostasis.

At the hotel restaurant, facing Red Square, my luncheon companions were a French businessman from Paris, a Brazilian doctor who specializes in arteriosclerosis, and a seventy-three-year-old Muscovite English professor. This latter spoke of the people's vitality in the Caucasus: "A man one hundred ten years old pretended to be only ninety because he wanted to remarry."

The Vladimir train was packed. At least half a dozen young people came and spoke with me. They knew a little English and were delighted to converse with a Canadian, with a priest. The three-hour journey passed quickly and enjoyably.

At the Vladimir station two other tourists and myself were greeted by a German-speaking Intourist guide. My generation of Russians knows more German than English. The present generation is anxious to learn English. At supper, I had the pleasure of meeting the two other tourists, Bob and Yvonne, foreigners like myself, and very much in love. I sensed that she was Catholic and that he was not. I sensed that they were not married. Both were deeply interested in the Russian tradition. We spoke of Archbishop Bloom, of Rublev and his glorious Trinity, of Berdyaev, of sobornost (oneness). We spoke of Christ and of God's love for every person. I gave them each a medal of Our Lady of Combermere.

I found the Vladimir hotel much better than the high-class National in Moscow. I had a big cozy room equipped with TV and radio. The atmosphere breathed peace and quiet. It was a real rest after the noise and hustle of Moscow!

Speaking of television, some very good programs originate from Moscow and cover the whole Soviet Union. Everyday one can enjoy some of the world's best ballet, operas, folk singing and dancing, fairy tales and cartoons. What an education in art the young people of Russia are getting through this medium. But television anywhere in the world comes at a price. In North America we have to suffer commercials; in the Soviet Union it's political speeches.

After breakfast the next morning, Bob, Yvonne and I were greeted by a rather extraordinary guide. He introduced himself simply as Sasha. I think of him as "saintly" because he has such a love for people, for the gut-level roots of his own people, for the soil which gave him birth. We spent all day with him visiting old Russia. Earlier, I had offered Mass privately in my room. The gospel had reminded me that if you have a little faith you can do anything. The day was gray, so I prayed for a sunny day. My heart was heavy about Bob and his beautiful Yvonne. Evidently they loved one another; yet, why were they not married? Yvonne especially struck me as hurt by the irregularity of their relationship. I asked God "to do something."

We left Vladimir for Suzdal some thirty kilometers away to see and touch the buildings, the ways, the traditions of old Russia.

Four kilometers from Suzdal we drove slowly through a truly old-fashioned Russian village: one street, not too long, flanked on either side by colorful wooden houses. The street led to a church courtyard which contained the traditional three buildings: a highly decorated, large, unheated, summer church; a smaller, heated but undecorated winter church; and a tower overlooking the Nerl River. This complex had been built in the twelfth century by Prince Yuri Longarm. During one period of his life he lived there and got his revenue by exacting a passage tax from all ships on their travels between Suzdal and Moscow.

Suzdal itself became a great center of Russian power and culture during the twelfth century. Today it is being developed as a showplace of old Russia. There, you find some marvelous wooden churches, isbahs and windmills.

Museums abound, displaying wooden and iron tools and weapons, and colorful costumes. Founded in 1024, Suzdal quickly developed as a principality and as an educational center. At one time it boasted one of the finest schools of iconography in Russia, famous especially for its Icons of Tenderness. Its influence lasted until the end of the seventeenth century.

We visited an isbah (or peasant's house) made of logs. As you enter, you notice the unheated, summer living room. The winter room contains a spinning wheel, a cradle, icons in the east corner, a dining-room table, benches all around the walls, and a kitchen corner with utensils and wooden tools. The pride of the house is the stove. It is divided into three parts: the bottom where the poultry lived, the middle part which was used for cooking, and a huge oven on top of which the people slept. The richer the peasant, the fancier his stove and the fretwork outside his house.

We lunched with thousands of Russians in a *refectory*, which was the custom until very recently. We sat at a table extending from wall to wall. Waiters and waitresses wore national costumes. Diners here and there broke spontaneously into song. We had mede (honey wine) and a luscious borsch served in an earthenware tureen, with large wooden spoons, all ornamented.

The Monastery of the Savior, walled in, as are all monasteries in Russia, contains the Church of the Annunciation. Its apsed dome shines like silver in the sunset light. St. Euphemius founded this monastery in the fourteenth century. Other churches full of frescoes attracted pilgrims through the years. The most poignant fresco is the one of Our Lady holding the Child and surrounded by saints. It is entitled *"Everybody likes to see you"* (VSETJEBE YADU-JUTSJA). This monastery served at one time as a terrible political prison for bishops, priests and sectarians. Some had themselves buried alive, the more quickly to meet God.

Across from it, on the outskirts of the city, was the Gentle Convent of Intercession, also erected in the fourteenth century.

According to tradition, Andrew, a poor man, a fool for God (Yurodivi) saw Our Lady cover the city of Constantinople with her mantle to save it from the Turks. She has been seen many times protecting one city or another. Because of this, a custom grew of building a Church of the Intercession or a convent at the edge of cities to honor Mary's loving care.

The nuns here were reputed for their tenderness and gentleness. Some princes banished their wives to this convent for one reason or another. The first to be so banished is quite celebrated.

Vassily III Sogouroff, the Prince, wanted to marry. He had the five thousand most beautiful girls in Russia brought to him. He chose the most beautiful one. I saw her picture. Either it does not do her justice, or Vassily suffered from severe eye trouble, or women in those days needed a lot of help. Her name was Solomania. Unfortunately, since she was barren, he had her sent to the convent. She claimed to have been pregnant but that the child had died. When the child's grave was opened, they found only a doll. Vassily married a Polish princess who bore him Ivan the Terrible.

Suzdal's Kremlin contains the beautiful wooden Church of St. Nicholas (1766), the Cathedral of the Nativity (thirteenth century), and the Metropolitan's Palace, famous for its eighteenth-century reception room. Archbishop Hilarion tried to surpass the Moscow Patriarch's residence in luxury. His two stoves are most impressive. They are decorated with tiles, each with its own unique design. The Soviet government proposes to spend some sixty million rubles preserving and restoring the antiquities of Suzdal.

We returned to Vladimir, passing by many little villages

which reminded me of the novels of Gogol, Tolstoy and Dostoyevski. Vladimir was founded in 1108 by Vladimir Monomakh, the great Kievan ruler. As Kiev diminished in importance, Vladimir became the second capital of Russia. Alexander Nevsky was born and buried here. Kiev knew its greatest glory under Prince Andrei Bogolouvesky.

Vladimir made a heroic stand against the Tatar-Mongol attack of 1237. For four days, five thousand soldiers held at bay a hundred thousand Mongols. The city boasts a golden-gate church facing Kiev, St. Dmitri's Cathedral, whose outside walls are covered by thirteen hundred relief carvings; the Patriarchal Church of Our Lady's Dormition, which served as a refuge for the prince, his family, the archbishop, and others when the Mongols invaded the city. They set fire to the church and all died.

Sasha, our guide, directed us through crowds with great patience and humility. It was so good to be crushed among the Russians who gather here on weekends with such love and enthusiasm for their own roots.

At supper, a Leningrad professor of literature sat with me. He poured a little cognac into my glass. I told him that in my culture cognac was drunk after a meal. Undaunted, he poured some wine into the cognac, lifted his glass and exclaimed, "Leningrad cocktail." Bob and Yvonne arrived. We talked quite freely. The Russian professor noticed my cross. He reached inside his shirt and pulled out his cross. He told Bob and Yvonne that he and I were already friends. He exclaimed, "Here is the soul. In Canada are the vibrations (the memory) which emanate from the soul."

After supper Bob and Yvonne said, "We want to get married." I thanked God. We left the table, and I had the joy of witnessing for the Church their vows right there and then. I advised them to go through another marriage ceremony when they returned home, for the sake of civil law, canon law and their families. But I assured them that they were validly married. The Roman Catholic Church is a good mother who can make things easy for her children. They were very, very happy. So was I.

O yes! It had been a sunny day as well.

7. WARM HEARTS IN SIBERIA

Of course, it was only the middle of October, but I actually saw snow only *once* during my ten days in Siberia. Fellow tourists in Leningrad and Moscow had warned me, "Be sure to take warm clothing. The train is hardly heated at all. Get off at every stop. Go to the little shops (kiosks) at the station for food and drink. There is very little food available on the train, etc, etc."

I have always loved to travel by just about any conveyance—car, bus, plane, ship, train. I particularly enjoy ships and trains. They afford an opportunity for meditation and the gradual absorption of a new culture and new scenery.

The TransSiberian Railroad held a particular attraction for me, as for so many people of my generation. It is an ideal way of actually seeing and experiencing Russia. The "Pacific" takes seven days to cover the distance from Moscow to Novarosk, some ten thousand kilometers. Again I found the engineers competent and the roadbed quite smooth. The restaurant provided good borsch and steak at very decent prices. Its kitchen, though, would have benefited from a cleaning job, and also, its staff.

I shared a very satisfactory compartment with a young man from Switzerland, a judo expert on his way to Japan to perfect his art. Intourist highly publicizes the TransSiberian route from Europe to the Orient. For instance, I made friends with an elderly Norwegian gentleman on his way to America; a young Frenchman, a karate expert, was also going to Japan for further training.

For 48 hours—from Moscow to Novosibirsk, the capital of Siberia—I saw mostly thin trees, poor villages, shabby

58

cities, and some pasture fields with grazing cattle. It seemed to me that full-scale agricultural development is still a matter for the future. Except for a few miles of cultivated land close to the cities, there seemed to be very little grain growing, and very few gardens.

Siberia is immensely wealthy. It was conquered for Russia by Yermak, a Don Cossack, in 1582. Political prisoners and other condemned men were sent here to work the gold mines and the coal fields. Many of them suffered much under the most inhuman prison conditions. But most of them were either banished to villages where they were kept under surveillance, or soon released from prison and given the opportunity to settle in the same villages. Many became explorers; many developed the economic and cultural life of the area.

Canada could fit into Siberia with room to spare. Its population at present numbers only twenty-five million people. Gigantic power plants are being developed to supply electricity not only for the Soviet Union but also for foreign export. The USSR is self-sufficient in raw materials: iron ore for steel, gas, oil, diamonds, platinum, gold, coal, electricity and uranium. Siberia contains every mineral known to man.

For centuries its merchants developed the wealth which made European-Russia rich. These merchants built magnificent palaces in Irkutsk, in Moscow and in St. Petersburg. Siberian furs, especially sables, were famous all over the world. The silver-tipped sable is the most-prized fur coat in the world. There are only three in existence. They are owned by Happy Rockefeller, Sophia Loren, and Russia's only lady astronaut.

For several years now, the Soviet government has been offering special benefits to European-Russians to work in Siberia. You get a feeling that things are developing. Freight trains loaded with materials keep the railroad tracks busy. A lot of traffic is handled by the northern ports on the Arctic Ocean.

In Siberia, one easily understands the traditional enmity between China and Russia. Fear of the Chinese is, of course, an atavistic reflex. How can any Russian forget the constant invasions of his country by the Mongols through the centuries? How can he forgive their cruelty, torture and destructiveness? On the other hand, the Chinese lay claim to much of Siberian territory. God knows they need the space. By the year 2000 there will be over one billion Chinese, all contained within a territory half the size of Siberia. When they cast their eyes northward, what do they see? An empty land, huge, immense, beckoning with its wealth and its space. No wonder armies are drawn up on either side of the Amur River.

Western nations trembled when the USSR and the communist Republic of China became friends around 1950. Our fears were groundless. The mutual Russo-Chinese mistrust has such deep roots as to preclude the possibility of friendship between them. I prayed much for the healing of wounds as the train rolled on. Enmity anywhere hurts us all. Brotherhood cannot exist until all men are brothers.

My companion, the young Swiss, developed a severe headache, and was sick for two days. He spent most of his time sleeping. One afternoon he asked me to teach him poker, which I did. Medical services are easily available in the Soviet Union. As soon as the Swiss lad complained of sickness, I immediately notified the car attendant, a gracious and capable woman constantly at your service. At the very next stop a woman doctor came aboard, examined the young man, diagnosed his illness, and gave him the proper medication, gratis.

I felt that my presence was the main cause of his splitting headache. Early in the journey he told me that he believed in God and in God's care for him, but that he hated the Church and priests. He considered us greedy, money-grabbers. Gradually he seemed to lose some of his hostility. When I left the train at Novosibirsk, he got up, picked up my heavy bag, and insisted upon carrying it to the train platform. We shook hands warmly and parted friends. Before leaving, I gave him a medal of Our Lady of Combermere. He immediately put it on his key chain; I also gave one to the car attendant who said she would wear it, and who requested one for her girl friend.

As usual, an Intourist guide drove me to the hotel where I immediately contacted the director of Intourist. I wanted to meet specialists on cold-climate agriculture. Russian scientists have done a lot of research on the production of grains, vegetables and even fruits in Siberia. Since our own climate is slowly becoming colder and the growing season shorter, any information I might pick up could be of great value to our Madonna House farm which has to feed about a hundred people daily.

The Director was most cooperative, and instructed one of his guides to give me every possible cooperation. He was most curious to find out why a priest should be interested in agriculture. He couldn't have been more gracious had he been hired by the local bishop to take special care of a visiting Canadian priest.

At supper the maitre d' put me at a table with three other people. The restaurant was full. As usual, my entrance created a stir. I sat down and quietly asked my table companions if they spoke French or English. They didn't. But immediately three young men at the next table turned around and said, "We speak English. Come and sit with us."

I excused myself and moved to their table. Two were students, the third a painter. While we were eating, the artist sketched me. The result was amazing. He certainly had caught the essence: across my eye-glasses, in large letters was written "Kanada," and from my neck hung a huge cross with the *Pax Caritas* inscription. We became good friends. They wanted to meet again, and as I had already made plans for the next day, Friday, they agreed to return on Saturday.

I spent Friday afternoon doing research on agriculture at the State Public Scientific Technical Library of the Siberian branch of the Academy of the USSR, just a couple of blocks from my hotel; I was accompanied by Ludmilla, an Intourist guide. Although suffering from a severe cold, she assisted me all through the afternoon, which happened to be her afternoon off. "You are doing me a favor," she insisted, when I tried to persuade her to go home and rest. "You are keeping me occupied at something which I find very interesting."

She acted as interpreter for me with the library director, a very gracious and competent lady. We went through a series of articles, catalogues and books on the subject of cold-climate agriculture. Truly a profitable afternoon. The director promised to send me names and addresses of specialists in the field, as well as titles of books published in English on the subject. These I received shortly upon returning to Canada. I got in touch with "Information Canada" in Ottawa, which sent the director a number of Canadian publications on cold-climate agriculture. A nice reciprocal gesture, don't you agree?

Novosibirsk, the capital of Siberia, has a population of one and a half million people. Its buildings are new and the general feel of the city is one of youth, exuberance, enthusiasm and good health. The air is as pure as that of any city in the world, a little crisp perhaps but not for a Canadian. It is situated on the Ob River, known affectionately as "The Grandmother" because the Volga is the "Mother."

At the simple, large, wooden, active church that morning, I was able to pray with the people, divided into groups offering different prayers. Some were sharing in a Moleben, a service for a dead person. Others were singing the praises of the Mother of God. Still others were going around from icon to icon interceding for all mankind. I prayed especially for all prisoners and for those who had sent them to prison. I prayed for the inmates of concentration camps, past and present, and for their guards. I prayed for myself, so often an oppressor.

On Saturday, my friends, the artist and the two university students, took me to the botanical gardens by taxi. Everything was closed. The only person in the laboratory was the cleaning lady. The students explained to me how universities, schools, and most business places close down from Friday afternoon until Monday morning all over the Soviet Union. Since I wanted to ask the director a few questions, I suggested we telephone her. The cleaning lady rang her up; she answered that she would be over right away.

Dr. Zoe Nicolaivna Briantseva answered all my questions quickly and succinctly. I wanted titles of books dealing with cold-climate agriculture written in English, one or two in Russian for Catherine Doherty, and names of their top scientists in the field. The next day, Dr. Briantseva came to lunch at my invitation, and brought me two fine books written in Russian. She told me that she was on her way to a meeting with their top specialist on the subject, also a woman, Dr. K. A. Sobolevskaya, who teaches at The Academy of Agricultural Sciences in the University Town situated some twenty kilometers from Novosibirsk.

Just in case you're interested, you can order books and subscribe to magazines published in the Soviet Union simply by writing to:

The Union Publishing House, Moscow 308 USSR.

At supper, a pretty, intelligent young woman was seated at my table. She struck me as a very lonely person. The conversation gradually revealed she was. Although only twenty-three, she had already been married and divorced. Her head might be clear but her heart was bitter. "Woman," she pointed out, "has achieved equality in the Soviet Union but chivalry no longer exists. Twenty million men were lost in World War II. Women had to be self-reliant, to take care of the children by themselves, and engage in hard work." She longed for something better than merely material and sensual satisfaction. She seemed close to suicide. She was glad to talk to me, opening her heart without effort to a perfect stranger simply because he was a priest.

People need to see a priest who looks like a priest, who identifies himself. They are attracted to him like a magnet. They are stirred up. My pilgrimage in Russia turned out to be a working trip. People expect more from a priest here than do people anywhere else I have been. They want you to be different, to offer a possibility, to present a hope of something better than what they already know and experience. They long to see in your eyes a light, a brightness they somehow remember since they already have a spark of it in their own hearts.

To them a priest is like a memorial, a re-presentation, a walking "do this in memory of Me," a Liturgy incarnate in the restaurant, the street or the store. Literally thousands of people, perhaps millions, stopped and stared at my cross. Everyone saw it. A few kissed it. A few smiled. But thousands gasped, as if struck to the quick by a dart shot straight at their subconscious, awakening cherished memories which the regime had tried so hard to kill. Thank God, this girl left with hope.

After supper I watched TV for a while. Leonid Brezhnev, presently the strong man of the Soviet Union, appeared again. You see him nearly every day, mostly greeting delegations from various socialist countries, attending demonstrations, parading before large crowds. I grew to love him, thank God. He struck me as a kind of martyr (notwithstanding his own personal crimes). Daily he seemed more tired, more haggard. Several times he wept. When his mother died, he attended the funeral, which took place in the Church of the New Maidens Convent in Moscow. Ever since meeting Brezhnev via TV, I have prayed at every Mass for greater freedom in the Soviet Union, for a change of heart among the leadership, for a conversion also among capitalists and in my own heart.

8. SLUMBERING LAND AND LAKE OF FIRE

"Sibir," the Russian word for Siberia, means "Slumbering Land." It slumbers no more. Towns and cities have sprung up all over this immensity. The climate varies. Irkutsk, for instance, enjoys about the same climate as eastern Ontario, if slightly colder. Further north, of course, the lowest temperatures in the world have been recorded: ninety degrees below Farenheit. The Russians have quickly learned to build on the permafrost, to live in very cold climates, to dress accordingly. (Read Farley Mowat's exceptionally fine book entitled *Sibir*.)

Canadians have yet to realize the fact that they live in a northern country. We build houses and wear clothing which have more in common with the south than the north. To our everlasting shame, it was Americans from Florida who introduced the parka to us! I remember only too well the winter of 1942 in Edmonton, Alberta. There I was, dressed in light clothes, ordinary oxfords, my head covered only by a light felt hat, walking down the streets and freezing to death. I met these strange creatures wearing the old Eskimo parka which we had never even thought of adopting as proper winter dress. Farmers in western Canada dressed warmly in cold weather, but the city gentry froze heroically, or should I say stupidly.

Canadians are only vaguely aware of their immense northlands, which still need to be colonized, developed, respected and appreciated. The permafrost can be a friend as well as an enemy. If it's true that "in Rome you should do as the Romans do," it's equally true that in Canada we should learn to adapt to our land and to our environment. I visualize the day when a hundred million people will inhabit the Yukon, the Northwest Territories, the Hudson Bay area, Labrador, Victoria Island and Ellsmere Island. We could accommodate many more immigrants than we are doing at present, if we learned how to live in the north.

In this regard, Soviet scientists can teach us a lot. I pray that we will soon begin an exchange of competent scientists between our two countries. Unless we open our territories to our brothers and sisters knocking at our doors, we stand guilty before God and the human race. We are poor custodians of God's treasure—this immense land—entrusted to our care. Something sick and ridiculous has happened to us. We have lost all spirit of adventure and imagination.

We huddle in increasingly vast conglomerations situated no further than a hundred miles from the United States border. This insane phenomenon is on the increase. Within a few years ninety-percent of the Canadian population will be concentrated in ten major cities. Millions of square miles of God's earth clamor to be visited, cared for, transformed and utilized. In this matter our great enemies are fear and ignorance. It is scandalous that we should still be contending with each other: French and English, east and west, labor and capital. God knows we have better things to do, namely to unite in a common purpose: the glorious development of our vast territories for the benefit of immigrants as well as for our own benefit. Canada *has a national purpose* but few people are aware of it.

The contrast between Siberia's dynamic thrust and our pallid indifference brought tears to my eyes, tears that scalded my spirit. Rage, shame, frustration mingled with my cry to God for mercy upon us, for vision, for the same adventurous spirit our forefathers possessed. They opened the wilderness, the unknown, from east to west, from Atlantic to Pacific. Now it's up to us to open the wilderness from south to north, from the fiftieth parallel to the Arctic Ocean.

THE HUMBLED CHRIST IN RUSSIA

Irkutsk, capital of southeastern Siberia, a city of five hundred thousand people, was founded as a Cossack port in 1652, and became a town in 1686. When the Russians came, they found three principal native tribes of Mongolian origin. The Mongolian border lies only a few hundred miles to the south.

The Buryats lived in hectagonal log cabins. They were hunters and fishermen who ill-treated their women. Their favorite alcoholic drink was Kumiz, made from mare's milk. Today they have their own autonomous Republic. Their capital city, Ulan-Udi, means Brave Youth. It indicates the spirit and enthusiasm of the modern Buryat.

The Evenks lived in wigwams and claimed to be descendants of the bear, for which they have great veneration. The bear's paw hung in every wigwam as its principal charm. Mothers carried their babies in a back cradle. Should the baby fall out as she walked through the forest, she left it there, believing that its destiny was death. Old people were killed or simply allowed to die. These Evenks used deer skin for their clothing. They resembled many of our own native Canadians in customs and features. Semi-nomadic, they engaged in fur trapping, fishing and reindeer breeding. I saw one of their Shaman's suits: a leather dress totally covered with all kinds of iron, copper, leather amulets, bells and animal designs.

The Yakuts are the most numerous of the northern native people, numbering about half a million. They are chiefly lifestock breeders. Yakutsia covers more than one million square miles; the autonomous Republic was formed in 1922 with Yakutsk as its capital city. The area is rich in coal, iron ore, gold, diamonds, grain cultivation and fur trapping. The Soviet Union respects its native peoples.

From the seventeeth century until recent times, Irkutsk developed as Siberia's principal city. Political prisoners were banished here by the thousands. Many were incarcerated in Siberia's most infamous jail: the Alexandrovsky Central Prison, situated only twenty kilometers away. Dostoyevsky spent some years there, described in his famous novel *The House of the Dead*. The cells were too small for a man to stretch out fully. Always chained, the prisoners worked in the mines, wore thin clothes, ate slops, and slept on tiny cots with only a light blanket to protect them from the cold.

A number of Decembrists were exiled to Irkutsk or to the vicinity. The Decembrists, a group of rich noblemen, attempted to bring a measure of social justice to Russia in December, 1825, by staging a coup in St. Petersburg. They were caught by the Imperial police. Five of them were executed and the rest condemned to Siberia. In Irkutsk they developed the cultural and educational life of the city. Duke Valkonsky and his young wife (only nineteen years old when they arrived), devoted their whole lives to the people's welfare. The Intourist guide pointed out their palace with reverence. They are still remembered with affection by everybody.

Irkutsk, like every Russian city, has a fine public square. Three churches stand at one end, two Orthodox, and one Polish Catholic. All three are under repair, being restored to their original beauty. Poles exiled here in the nineteenth century built their own church. Some became famous explorers.

The Orthodox religion knew much success here from its very beginning. Its first bishop, St. Sophrony, has been canonized. In 1752 the local monastery had seven hundred fifty-two monks. It was destroyed during the 1917 revolution.

The TransSiberian Railroad was built in 1898, pretty much for the same reason as our own Canadian Pacific Railroad and at about the same time (1885): to bind the country together and to facilitate trade. The Soviet

Union's great man, and Siberia's most famous prisoner, Lenin, spent the years 1897 to 1900 in Shushunska village, near Krasnoyarsk, on Siberia's most important river, the Yenisey, 2,100 miles long. It was there, as a prisoner, that he came to appreciate the immense hydro-electric possibilities of the whole area.

God has richly blessed the Irkutsk region. All the natural elements and minerals can be found close by. Built in the middle of the Taiga (Wild Forest), it long enjoyed a thriving lumber industry. For years its houses and palaces were made of logs; there are still many beautiful, decorated log houses on its side streets. Some of them reminded me of Whitehorse, Yukon Territory.

The abundance of lumber was no surprise to me. I had long known that most of Siberia is an immense forest. The Taiga, the Wild Forests where huge trees grow and animals live freely, receded through the centuries, so that now it actually begins some one hundred miles east and north of Irkutsk. I was sorry to miss that, but I was amply rewarded by discovering the mineralogical museum at the University City, on the very outskirts of Irkutsk.

There, I saw treasures of jade, copper, silver, gold, huge graphite crystals as well as very dainty ones, apatite, marble of fifty different hues, malachite, onyx, a mineral named "Armstrong" after the first man (an American) to step onto the moon, placed side by side with another named "Gagarin," after the first man (a Russian) to orbit the earth. There was a variety of asbestos, of mica, and some fifty different kinds of precious stones. God is truly delightful. I praised him for all this beauty and for the fascinating shapes chiseled in so many huge rocks. There were roses, elephants, fish, birds and other shapes that I no longer remember. The most breathtaking was a landscape with men sitting around a campfire.

A group of students had come in and were being shown

around by the Director. As I was leaving he called me over, introduced me as a Canadian, and boldly punched me on the chest exclaiming "Be strong like a Siberian!" Automatically I punched him back, and said "Be strong like a Canadian!" I hate to brag, but he reeled back on his heels and everybody gasped. I grabbed his two hands, shook them warmly, thanked him profusely, and left with my guide. We laughed and laughed and laughed.

Now I'd like to tell you of something quite special God did for me on October 15th. On this day the Madonna House Apostolate, my spiritual family, celebrates its Foundation in Toronto in 1930 by Catherine de Kolyschkine, of whom I have spoken several times.

I wanted to visit Lake Baikal, Siberia's jewel, some fifty miles away. Intourist had told me on the previous evening to come to their office at nine o'clock the following morning. I did, only to be informed that there were no cars or guides or chauffeurs available for the Baikal trip that morning. Everything had already been booked. The trip cost forty-one dollars, a large sum for me, but I couldn't bear the thought of being so close and missing the glories of this Lake. One of the clerks mentioned that a Canadian lady had hired a private car. Perhaps she would take me with her. Shyly I approached the lady, Mrs. Jeanette McDermott, from Toronto. We already knew each other since we had met at supper the night before. Most graciously she acceded to my request: "Father, it will be a joy and an honor to have you with me." Minutes later I was riding in a luxury car with a charming Torontonian, a competent guide, an expert chauffeur—and all for free, thanks to the goodness of God, the tenderness of Our Lady, and the kindness of Mrs. McDermott.

On this simply glorious day, the air was soft and fresh, the sun shone freely on everything, and the road led through a forest of birch, larch, and ever-

71

greens. Pavel, our guide, told us the legend.

Father Baikal had 336 sons, that is, the streams and rivers which flow into the Lake. He had one daughter, Angara. Father Baikal was known for his fits of temper: each year the lake is shaken by some two thousand earthquakes. One night, he flew into his usual rage, only this time he really blew his gasket! The storm raged all over the Lake, accompanied by thunder and lightning, the likes of which have never been seen before or since. Baikal evidently was having a ball.

His daughter, Angara, had long been secretly in love with Yenisey and was biding her time to run to her lover, who waited miles away. That night she broke out and rushed passionately to the embrace of Yenisey. That's how the great river Angara, the only one to flow out of the Lake, was born. When Father Baikal discovered her escape, he took a huge stone and threw it at the spot through which she had flowed away. I saw the tip of that rock. It is called "the Shaman Rock."

Lake Baikal is the deepest lake in the world, some six thousand feet deep. It is twenty million years old, possibly the oldest lake in the world. As an inland water body its volume is second only to either the Black Sea or the Caspian. It is six hundred thirty-six kilometers long and eighty kilometers at its widest. Mountains surround it; some, in the south, rise up to six thousand feet. Its fauna and flora number more than eighteen hundred species. Every natural chemical element is found in the area, including scores of minerals and gem stones. Fish abound in its waters. The cherished sturgeon and the omul, a fish similar to salmon, are among its finest. At lunch we were served raw omul.

Now raw meat and especially raw fish "ain't at all" my cup of tea. But I could dine on raw omul every day. Russia's favorite fish is the sturgeon. We had some for lunch, straight from the Lake. All over the Soviet Union, sturgeon is the highest priced item on the menus, except in Irkutsk, where it is the cheapest. Needless to say I ate sturgeon every day.

I shall always remember the golden atmosphere mingling with Baikal's blue waters. I shall always praise God for those refreshing hours. I shall always hold in kind remembrance Jeanette, Pavel and my chauffeur.

Baikal means "fire." On our Foundation Day, I prayed that we might be on fire with love for God, every single person and everything that exists. I prayed that my complacency would often be shaken by inner earthquakes as Lake Baikal is every year.

9. POINTERS FOR PILGRIMS

It is wise to be identified as a priest. Young people want to find out about you. Others know exactly where you stand. On the whole, you are treated with more consideration.

Canadians are popular in Russia right now. We are no threat to any nation. Our climate and geography have much in common with the Soviet Union's.

Be careful when you cross a street unless you have made a recent will and just seen a priest. The only sure way to make it across alive is to hang on to the coat tails of one, preferably two Russians. Every time I tried it on my own, I had to rush back to the sidewalk to avoid being squashed by a dozen trucks out to get *me* personally. The pedestrian has no rights, so beware!

You can get into any museum for less than fifty cents if you go on your own.

Hippies are extremely rare. I saw one hippie, a girl. She was pointed out to me by a Russian as a serious anomaly.

Russians love to exchange gifts. Bring some "souvenirs" if you visit Russia. The most desired souvenirs are records of popular music, preferably soft rock. Pictures, postcards from your native country, ball-point pens, felt-tipped pens and nylons make acceptable presents.

In Russia, do as the Russians do. They are different, vastly different. Love them and you will get to know them. Their culture, their ways are very rich in meaning. Russians are at their best enjoying ballet, opera, and the circus. There they are truly themselves. They love the beautiful. Professed atheists stand in admiration before the graceful churches of Russia, her icons and old frescoes.

No one ever talks politics, criticizes the government or mentions concentration camps. Yet, all are aware that much is not well within their own country. One could ask the question, "In which country of this world are all things well?"

Expect to line up for everything. The lines move fast.

The Russians I met ate a lot, three times a day, and drank a lot of beer, vodka, cognac and champagne. They adore sturgeon, but they also eat much meat, potatoes, bread and soup. Meals in Russia cost about one-third the price you pay for the same meal in America.

There is an anti-vodka drinking campaign going on at the present time.

Consumer goods are being produced in abundance. You can get just about anything in the stores.

The post-office service is exceptionally fast and reliable. To send a parcel home, simply go to a post office. A clerk will wrap the parcel for you and address it. The cost of surface mail is very cheap. All my parcels reached Canada within six weeks of mailing.

Bookstores abound. One-fourth of all books printed in the world are published in the Soviet Union.

Lenin is everywhere: statues, streets and buildings are named after him, and there are countless displays of his books. Karl Marx follows him in popularity.

Arrange your itinerary in full before leaving your own country. Intourist detests making any change of program for tourists after they have arrived in the Soviet Union.

The Caucasian mountains in Georgia are considered the cradle of the Aryan races. The Slavs first left there for Bulgaria, then went to Kiev, Novgorod and Suzdal. The *Basques* also originate from the Caucasus, from an area called Iberia. (Read Lermontov on the Caucasus.)

In case of difficulty, go directly to the Intourist director at your hotel, to the car attendant on the train or to your floor supervisor at your hotel. They are very efficient.

The menus I saw were just about identical all over Russia. Steak being the cheapest item on the menu, needless to say a Canadian has no trouble practicing "holy poverty!" Salads contain mainly fish or meat.

Lenin's real name is V. I. Ulanov. He chose to be called "The man from the Lena," although he spent his time as a prisoner in Siberia near the Yenisey, and not the Lena.

Soft black caviar costs about five dollars an ounce, but it is delicious.

My cross with its inscription "Peace and Love" pleased many, many people. Each person to whom I gave a medal of Our Lady of Combermere received it with true joy.

All hotels are well-supplied with toilet paper, soap and large towels.

Your bed consists of a bottom sheet and a double top sheet with an opening through which a warm, thick blanket is inserted. Your one pillow measures about three feet square and is very comfortable. The sheet-blanket is not tucked in under the mattress. It is merely tucked under itself. You slip into it and quickly learn to sleep cosily that way.

Upon arrival at a hotel you will be asked to hand over your passport and visa. They will be returned, either immediately, the next day or when you are about to leave.

As a pilgrim, I carried a small icon of Our Lady in my breast pocket. I also brought one of St. Nicholas with me. He is the pilgrim's traditional companion. He accompanies Christ as the Lord visits the poor and the suffering. St. Nicholas' popularity is second only to that of the Mother of God. Russians love him for his gentleness, kindness and generosity.

Doctors are easily available. So are druggists.

I drank mostly mineral water or fruit water because of my susceptibility to diarrhea. For diarrhea the best pill I found in Russia was Enterocoptol, about one cent each.

The electric current is two hundred twenty volts everywhere. I had brought a condenser with me. It proved invaluable for heating water and also for my heating pad, but was useless for my electric razor.

Icon prints and postcards are impossible to find. I searched and asked everywhere. By accident, I found some Rublev icon slides and another box of icon slides in a little shop. In Suzdal I finally found an extraordinary book of icons.

Bring envelopes or scotch tape. Local envelopes have no glue.

The highest university degree is Member Correspondent; next Academician, then Doctor, then Candidat. The lowest is Engineer.

Do not buy antiques from individuals. Generally they are not authentic.

Ballet achieves a spiritual discipline of the muscles. It reveals all the beauty of the human body, its immense gracefulness. It calls for a man and a woman who respond perfectly to each other, who together in some way represent the love that exists in God. Ballet is pure—man striving to be as beautiful as God made him.

Women keep Russia clean. At four in the morning you see the Matushkas sweeping the sidewalks, the squares, the parks, washing everything clean, making the world a place worthy of mankind.

The Matushkas fill the churches, intercede for all, and protect Orthodoxy.

Paperclips can be useful.

Don't spend all your time with fellow tourists. Allow God to reveal to you his wonderful works among the Russian people.

Rushing everywhere gets you nowhere. Take time to reflect, to ponder and to pray. God is with you and he will take care of you.

If you wear dentures, bring some Polident. My teeth got

black every few days. Polident cleans them up in no time.

Now for a word about proper behavior in a store. One: Find the item you want to buy. Two: Get its price. Three: Go to the cashier closest to where your item is displayed. Four: Tell her the price and pay her. Five: She will give you a little ticket. Six: Take the ticket to the clerk standing behind the counter where your item is to be found. Seven: She will wrap it up and hand it over to you. The interesting part about all this is that each step means standing in line. A line-up forms as soon as you decide that you want something. A foodstore is called a Gastronom.

Russians walk quickly, in a bee line, moving straight ahead. It's simply amazing how few collide.

Everything in Russia is different, simply everything.

Each city has its own personality and its own rhythm.

Russians are very proud of their invincibility as evidenced by the 1812 defeat of Napoleon, and their victory in World War II, which they call, "The Great Patriotic War."

The air fare from Moscow to Irkutsk is one-third cheaper than the train fare.

If you want to attend church service simply ask time and directions at the Intourist desk.

A pilgrim is a person who needs to touch the holy, to be on a spot where God manifested himself in a special way. As he discovers the presence of God in holy places and in his brothers, he becomes aware of that same presence within himself. He discovers the temple, the sacred place of his own heart, where God—Father, Son and Holy Spirit—have made their home. He prostrates before them. He adores. He intercedes. He asks for mercy.

> I am going to see that Head which was
> crowned with thorns, and that Face
> which was spit upon for me.

Pointers for Pilgrims

I have loved to hear my Lord spoken of;
    and wherever I have seen the print
    of His shoe, there I have coveted
    to set my foot too.

His name has been to me a civet-box:
    yea, sweeter than all perfumes.

His voice has been most sweet; and His
    Countenance I have more desired
    than the light of the sun.

His words I did use for my food, and for
    strength against my weakness.

He has held me, and hath kept me from my
    sins; yea, He has strengthened my
    steps in His way.

        —Bunyan's "Pilgrim's Progress"

10. GREAT RUSSIA

Great Russia, with its center in Moscow, comprises two-thirds of the Soviet Union, and contains more than one-half of its population. After Kiev, it was here that the national character was formed long before the national state took shape.

Four thousand years before Christ, the ice mass which covered nearly all of the present-day U.S.S.R. began to recede, leaving behind huge bodies of water: the Black Sea, the Caspian Sea, Lake Ladoga near Leningrad, Lake Ilmen near Novgorod, Lake Baikal near Irkutsk, deep in Siberia, and a magnificent series of waterways. For centuries the rivers and lakes were the main roads of one-sixth of the earth's land surface.

The original Slavs came from the Pamir mountains in Northern Tibet, the cradle of the Aryan races. Around 2300 B.C., two main groups of tribes began their Western march, pushed on by invaders. The Nordic tribes settled first of all around the Black Sea and the Caspian Sea in Southern Russia. Through the centuries they moved west to become the ancestors of the Ukrainians, Poles, Latvians, Lithuanians, and many more nations.

The Great Russians—so named by the Byzantines in the thirteenth century as they grew in importance—belong to the second group of tribes which migrated from the Pamirs some 4,300 years ago, namely (hold on to your hats, folks) the *Kelts*! The Slav Kelts first settled in the Priapet marshes west of the Dnieper River. They wanted privacy and solitude. They got it. No conqueror for centuries coveted their homeland. It was there, until 500 A.D., that the national character continued to be formed. Other Kelts moved on westward to give birth to the Irish, Scottish, Welsh, Britons, and perhaps the Basques, who settled for a time in "Iberia" of the Caucasus.

Thus for more than two thousand years the Slav Kelts knew very little foreign influence. The strong self-identity that strikes us in every Russian we meet, like Trefoil, forged deep roots in their subconscious during this long incubation period in the marshes.

When they migrated to the Upper Volga forest regions of Eastern European-Russia, beginning in the sixth century A.D., they were already in tune with nature. They radiated a fortitude forged by thousands of years of harsh mountain and marsh life. They possessed traditions, myths, stories, songs, and a rich animistic religion. Like all Kelts, they believed in spirits—the spirit of the river, the rainbowed spirits of the forest, the spirit of the house, the spirit of the oven. Most of these were friendly and showered with gifts, but some were evil and had to be appeased by rituals.

Like the Chinese, they had a great reverence for their ancestors, as well as for their living parents. To this day, the spirits of their deceased are believed to reside in the icon corner as well as in Heaven. "A wise man," goes a proverb, "praises his father and his mother. A fool praises his wife." Perun, the god of thunder and lightning, was highly honored among them. They worshiped many other gods. In the gray earth-forest of Northeast European-Russia the Keltic Slavs came to maturity and acquired a rich, varied and unconquerable character.

Sobornost, that is, oneness of mind and heart, together-ness, was born here, even before Christ manifested himself. Life in the forest required that all men work together. Together they cut trees. Together they built houses. Together they cleared land for agriculture, mostly by burning, to enrich the poor gray soil with charcoal. They

81

grew rye, oats, wheat and vegetables, mostly cabbage and beets. Many became dairy farmers, and cultivated hay to feed their animals. To this day a Russian has a particular fondness for a neat haystack.

They came to know and love the *forest*. They listened to the forest, to each tree, and made friends with it. The Slav "feels" the forces of nature, even as our own North American Indians do. He bowed before the mighty oak to acquire its strength. The oak reminded him of man; in the birch he honored the beauty of women and their fertility. Gay dances took place around the white birch in early spring.

The forest was a friend. It taught him. It offered protection. Here one could hide from the enemy. By the time he was three years old, a child had learned to wander safely through the enchanting woods. He broke twigs as a guide for his return from delightful adventures.

Trees offered their heat as protection from the cold in the isbah. Birch bark served many purposes: kindling for the fire; material for shoes (lapti), cups, plates, writing and decorations.

In a region subject to extreme temperatures of hot and cold, hospitality meant survival. The stranger was welcomed with bread and salt in the poor man's isbah (heated house), and with more lavish foods in the rich peasant's home.

The forest provided animals for meat and their furs for warm clothing. But its prize treasures were wild honey and mushrooms. Honey brought sweetness to a hard life, and honey wine (mede) rejoiced the heart and warmed a cold body.

According to legend, *the bear, symbol of Russia,*had once been a man to whom hospitality was refused. Like the Slav himself, the rejected bear took refuge in the forest and there competed with man for its treasures, honey and berries. The Russian identifies with the bear. Since time immemorial he has competed with him, literally wrestled with him, captured him and played with him. To a Russian, a bear means wrestling, conquest, circus and fun.

Crafts of all kinds occupied the long winter months. Many towns and villages were famous for some speciality: Tver for shoes; Yaroslavl for its linens; Tula for samovars.

"Collect your *folklore*," said Gorki, some decades ago, "the better to know your past and to be who you are." A century before, Pushkin had remarked, "What a delight these tales are." The great Russian composers, Rimsky-Korsakov, Mussorgsky, Borodin, Glinka, Stravinsky, Tchaikovsky took their inspiration from stories which had become popular during Great Russia's Middle Ages. Stories, legends, myths had been passed down from generation to generation for centuries, especially by the grand-mothers, the "batushkas." Deeply, deeply these stories penetrated the national unconscious. From the tenth to the thirteenth centuries, whole new professions developed: troubadours, jesters, professional beggars, wailers for funerals, performers for weddings, and the revered pilgrims with their limitless variety of all-absorbing religious tales. These people had a tremendous influence in forming the Russian spirit and culture.

Christianity, which had come to Kiev in 988, was quickly brought to the forest people. They received Christ with great joy because the same God is the Father of existing nature and of our radiant Lord, Jesus Christ. Quickly they transferred to St. Michael, to St. George, to Christ, the attributes they had venerated in Perun. After Jesus and Mary, they honored St. Nicholas for his mercy. Sobornost, hospitality, ritual were not rejected, but rather transfigured by the power of the risen Lord and lifted up to share in his glory. They truly became a "new creation." Rarely in the history of mankind has Christ taken flesh so eagerly in an already existing human culture. Like Mary, Russia said her Fiat, received the Son of God in her womb, and became Holy Russia, herself a Bogodoritza, she-who-gave-birth-to-God. He purified her and made her his own.

Music, painting, legends now centered upon Christ, upon his Mother Mary—She-who-gave-birth-to-God—the angels, the saints. Architecture turned its love and talents to building graceful churches and chapels whose fiery domes and crosses reach out to meet the cross and fire which come down from heaven.

Herein lies the secret of the Russian's quest for the absolute. Each one of us is blest and also "suffers" from the magi syndrome: a star shines somewhere within us and draws us, if only we don't obscure it with arrogance or selfishness. Thousands of people in Russia became pilgrims, following a star, a star that led them to the discovery of the incarnate and glorious Christ *in each person.* It led them to various other places where God had manifested himself in a striking way, where holy people had met God and shared him with their disciples. Eventually, because God is God, they too became a holy spark of Christ's living fire and light, for the warmth and joy of all men and women, their other selves.

The *music* of the Russian Orthodox Church comes from the Holy Spirit singing in the depths of our being. The Byzantines heard him and sing with him—they still do. The Jews also. Russian modes groan and praise with the Holy Spirit. It is a music which soothes the wounds of the human spirit, lifts it up with all its sorrows and yearnings to the Father, and bows low before his transcendent majesty. A music like none other, it pulses with our blood and beats in the ocean rhythm with our primordial matrix. At a liturgical service, something deep within you awakens, your whole being unfolds to joy, you are comforted. Spontaneously you praise God.

Orthodoxy *satisfies all the senses*: smell, sight, hearing. It draws the emotions and the spirit into prayer. Its healthy exercises of low bows and prostrations caress the *body*. Guilt dissolves as one repeats over and over again: "Lord have mercy, Lord have mercy, Lord have mercy." The Russians—as you and I—longed for a loving and merciful God. And he came to them. They have been spared Puritanism and Jansenism. But they have always known their personal guilt and yearned for forgiveness and for transformation. They long to become fire and light. God revealed himself to them as fire and light.

With Orthodoxy, Constantinople introduced *icons*. Typically, the Russians developed their own styles and many schools of iconography. Some of the most celebrated took shape between the eleventh and sixteenth centuries in Great Russia. Most famous are the schools of Novgorod, Yaroslavl, Pskov and Moscow. The Moscow school had its center some fifty miles north, in what became the country's most celebrated monastery, the Trinity Lavra of St. Sergius, founded around 1350. Andrei Rublev was a monk there. In the early 1400s he painted the world's most famous Iconostasis—the first, I think—in the Moscow Kremlin Cathedral of the Annunciation. He painted hundreds of icons, his most beautiful being the loving Trinity.

The iconographer, after much prayer and fasting, reveals the glory of God hidden in everything that exists: the chair you sit on right now, the things you see, your own self, in every person, especially the saints, more so in She-who-gave-birth-to-God, and most especially in the glorious Christ. "Christ is so extraordinary that everything else becomes ordinary." Before an icon, one says little, if anything at all. One listens. If one is patient, hungry for God, quiet inside, the icon will "speak," revealing God, his mercy, forgiveness, tenderness, majesty, but most of all, *his love.*

The Great Russians lived for centuries more or less isolated, listening to nature, struggling for life, cherishing their identity. Then they were put to the test by Mongols, by Tatars (Turkish-Mongols) and by many other providential forces. Often persecuted, sold as prized slaves in all the world's principal markets, pillaged and ruined century after century, they learned to remain themselves and cherish their personal ideals. These influences and ideals are impossible to put into words, even for a Great Russian. They are premodal, atavistic, gut-level stuff. Yet because of all this, a Russian possesses a rich, subconscious culture which has resisted all enemies. It has assimilated *them* and become unconquerable.

The great Napoleon, defeated at Borodino in 1812, acknowledged: "Today Russia has earned the right to call itself unconquerable." But Russia is greater than he—She was invincible centuries before Napoleon's birth. Her identity is so strong that no one has been able to change her, not even her own tsars or westernizing philosophers.

Today the Soviet Union is ruled by technology and materialism. They are merely the oppressors of the moment. They will not conquer Russia. No oppressor ever has. She will eliminate what in them doesn't fit and assimilate what does. Such has been her history for four thousand known years and more.

11. IT'S A FACT (RUSSIAN)

It was time to return to Moscow. I was sitting in the visitors' lounge at the Iskutsk airport waiting for departure time. Coffee tables were loaded with free Soviet literature. I learned the following things, browsing through the many booklets put out by Novisti Press of Moscow:

— Lenin was the greatest man that ever lived.

— Karl Marx was madly in love with his wife.

— One-third of the people in the Soviet Union are students.

— Fifty million citizens receive a pension. Old-age pension for men begins at sixty, for women at fifty-five. People engaged in dangerous occupations stop working at an earlier age and receive adequate compensation.

— Lenin was the greatest man that ever lived.

— Marriage should be for love. When love no longer exists, divorce is advised.

— The Chinese have many things wrong with them.

— The Soviet Constitution guarantees the following rights and privileges: the right to work, to have an education, and to disability care; free medical care, freedom of conscience, freedom of expression, leisure time; the right to assembly, street demonstrations and personal property; privacy of correspondence and a guarantee of the inviolability of the person and the home.

— Lenin was the greatest man that ever lived.

— Fifteen million people belong to the Communist Party; ninety-eight million are members of trade unions; the Komsomol, the youth organization, numbers thirty-two million.

— "Whitsuntide Shakers" (better known to us as Holy

87

Rollers) are not allowed in the Soviet Union.

— Lenin was the greatest man that ever lived.

— Eighteen is the minimum age for marriage. Each spouse is free to keep one's own name or change to the other's surname. In matters of property, they have equal rights.

— The Soviets insist on peace for all men, freedom, fraternity.

— Socialism grows while capitalism declines.

— Lenin is the greatest man that ever lived.

— In 1917, eighty-percent of Russians were farmers, less than twenty-percent workers. The reverse is now true.

— Education, culture, science, development, production are providing a happy, full life for all.

— Never a word anywhere about oppression, concentration camps, Solzhenitsyn.

— Lenin was the greatest man that ever lived.

Our jet landed in Omsk after three and a half hours of non-stop flight. I noticed that the land within a radius of fifty miles or so around the city was cultivated. Immense areas in Siberia await eventual agricultural development.

At Omsk, a genial Intourist guide boarded the plane to greet me. He led me straight to the foreign visitors' lounge and restaurant where I enjoyed a modest snack in lonely splendor. I tried to get to the restroom. I should have known better. The cleaning lady had chosen the precise moment of our arrival to wash up with thoroughness and enthusiasm—the area right in front of the bowls! Men were lined up for half a block. I returned quietly to the lounge.

From Omsk to Moscow, at sunset, we traveled in a roseate glow. For 5,800 kilometers—the distance between Irkutsk and Moscow—it was my great joy to call God's blessing upon all the people and the land over which we flew. I blessed the waters, the fields, the forests. I blessed each person in the name of the Father, of the Son, of the

Holy Spirit. The Jesus prayer "Lord Jesus Christ, Son of the living God, be merciful to me a sinner"—sprang from my heart constantly to embrace, console and soothe all. I poured out over them the oil and the balm flowing from the heart of Catherine Doherty, of my Madonna House family, and of the hundreds of people all over the world who were praying, sacrificing, loving, as they went about their daily tasks and as I pilgrimed in their name.

"Father of our Lord Jesus Christ," I said, "I adore you in each person. I believe in your glorious presence in nature and in all things. I adore you living within the humble home of my poor heart. Have mercy on us all. Let us be still and know that you are our God. Like Jesus, let us really believe in the awesome fact that each one of us is your beloved and cherished son or daughter. Father, change our hearts—my heart—from selfishness to love, from restlessness to peace, from anger to tenderness. You have made all things beautiful and good for us. All things belong to each one of us. Send with power your Holy Wisdom, the Lord Jesus himself, to take full possession of each one of us and of everything that exists. May we be renewed and transformed, all together, united in an immense sobornost from which *no one* or *nothing* is excluded. Someday, with one voice, led by Jesus, by the Holy Spirit and Mary, may we say, 'Our Father, who art in heaven, hallowed be thy name. Thy kingdom come. Thy will be done on earth as it is in heaven.' "

Just before beginning our descent, the rosy clouds formed themselves into delicate figures reminiscent of Japanese painting. It seemed like hundreds of pilgrims, row after row, had come to greet us, and to remind us of the fact that we, too, some day would live in fullness of glory.

Moscow was densely overcast. We came down, visibility zero. I had been anxious to see the city from the air, but not a glimmer of light came through the opaque clouds.

The first lights I saw were parallel to the eye and we touched down, immediately, in the rain. A car came up to the plane when we had stopped. An Intourist young woman gathered me and my bags and packed me off to the hotel in a matter of minutes. I felt like a visiting foreign dignitary! Somebody mentioned the special treatment I was getting. Foolishly I put my finger to my lips and said, "I'm Mikarios. I shaved my beard."

This may be the place to insert a very summary history of Russia with particular emphasis on Moscow.

2300 B.C.—The Nordic tribes and the Kelts move westward from India.

700 B.C.—The Iranians come and intermingle with other tribes.

375 A.D.—The Huns cross the Volga. The Great Migration begins.

862 A.D.—Rurik, the Norse, is invited by Slav tribes warring against each other to unite them by becoming their ruler. Novgorod, first capital city.

911 A.D.—Oleg, son of Rurik, chooses Kiev as the capital of the Rus.

988 A.D.—St. Vladimir I adopts Christianity.

1019-1054—Yaroslavl the Wise, Kiev's greatest prince. He built St. Sophia, wrote the first code of law, established many cities.

1037—Kiev becomes the See of the Metropolitan Archbishop of the Russian Orthodox Church.

1054—Catholic-Orthodox schism.

1113-1125—Vladimir Monomakh, a great Kievan ruler.

1139-1174—Prince Andrei Bogolubsky, son of Yuri Dolgoruki, rules in Suzdal and consolidates northeast Russia.

1147—Moscow is first mentioned in the records. Prince Yuri Dolgoruki, son of Vladimir Monomakh, is considered its founder. He built a kremlin out of wood. Moscow was founded to protect northeast Russia, Suzdalia.

1200-1600—Numerous invasions by the Swedes, Mongols, Tatars, Poles, Lithuanians, Germans.

1252-1263—Alexander Nevski defeats the Swedes and makes a pact with the Mongols.

1325—The Metropolitan See is moved from Suzdal to Moscow.

1324-1341—Prince Kalita (Moneybags) becomes ruler of Moscow, and an agent for the Tatars. Russia begins to revive.

1350—St. Sergius founds the Trinity Monastery to unite the people of Russia.

1380—Prince Dmitri Donskoi defeats the Tatars at Kulikovo.

1462-1505—Ivan III, the Great, lifts the Tatar yoke, fights off the Lithuanians and adds Novgorod to Moscow.

After the fall of Constantinople to the Turks in 1453, Moscow becomes known as the *third Rome*, a strong Temptation.

1533-1584—Ivan IV, the Terrible, builds St. Basil and other beautiful churches, destroys the Tatar remnants in Kazan and Astrakhan, sends Yermak to conquer Siberia. He was awesome and cruel.

1584-1598—Fedor, the last Rurik; Russia's population at that time is about fifteen million.

1589—Moscow becomes a Patriarchate.

1598-1605—The unhappy reign of Boris Godunov.

1604—The appearance of "false Dmitri," which begins the "time of troubles," a period which ends in 1613 with the election of the Romanov family to the throne. The Romanov Dynasty ruled until 1917.

1682-1725—Peter the Great conquers over the Turks and the Swedes, regains much territory, builds St. Petersburg. Industry begins.

1762-1796—Catherine II, the Great.

1801-1825—Alexander I defeats Napoleon in 1812. A tradition has it that Alexander abdicated and went to live as a hermit (a staretz) in Siberia to atone for the *sins committed by people in authority*. When the Soviets opened his tomb in the 1920s, they found it empty.

1861—The emancipation of the serfs.

19th Century—The classical period of Russian Literature and Music.

1867—Sale of Alaska to the United States of America.

1905—A peasant demonstration led by Fr. Gapon turned into "bloody Sunday."

1917—The Bolshevik October Revolution.

12. PRAYING FOR MOSCOW

My last five days in the Soviet Union were spent in Moscow. Intourist allowed me one day in Zagorsk, some fifty miles northeast, the center of the Russian Orthodox Church since the late fourteeth century. But more about that later.

I'm not exactly what you call a prayerful person. I don't pass long hours in church. As a matter of fact, week days I'm all in favor of a twenty or twenty-five-minute Mass. Sunday, when we celebrate Christ's resurrection, my devotion, by the grace of God, can extend up to one hour, but not much more than that.

It was, therefore, something of a private miracle when, moment by moment, and day by day, all I *wanted* to do in Moscow was to pray. People suggested the ballet, the circus and other wonderful distractions. Much as I love ballet and am enchanted by a circus, much as I enjoy tours, at this particular time of my life prayer became the sole attraction of my heart.

The Red Square and the Kremlin beckoned to me daily. I walked all around the grounds saying the fifteen mysteries of Mary's rosary, which recall the principal scenes of our redemption. I blessed every person, every building, every vehicle I met. Following the Byzantine-Russian Orthodox tradition, it was an immense thrill for me to bless the waters of the Moscow River flowing by the Kremlin—the seat of government. I dropped into its waters a holy crucifix, given to me by a saint some years ago, and with which I had bléssed many persons, many things, with which I had performed a number of private exorcisms.

Holy objects, like this crucifix, carry within themselves

a special presence of God with power to repel evil, to sanctify creation, to transform the cosmos. Thus do we give back to God that part of his creation which sin stole from him. Every Christian, every Jew or Muslim or Buddhist, every person who believes in God and loves him, goes about the world sanctifying everything he touches, everyone he meets, making it ready for the second coming of Christ—the Parousia—when Christ will be all in all. I firmly believe that the waters flowing over my crucifix in the Moskva River receive from it a blessing, a power to dispel evil and bring salvation to everything: man, animals, vegetables, minerals, machines, houses, buildings and anything else they touch, making them beautiful for God.

As I pilgrimed inside the Kremlin walls, passing the Hall of Congresses, the National Assembly, thousands of tourists, guards and policemen milling about the grounds, I bowed low interiorly before God's presence within each person and each thing. I recognized the glory of Christ, the image of the Father, the tenderness of the Holy Spirit in the policeman, in the guard, in the tourist, bringing to life and strengthening the bond among us which God has already put there. Someday there will be a new heaven and a new earth. All things will shine like the transfigured Christ on Mount Tabor. Like the Apostles looking at Christ at the moment of his transfiguration, we too shall be amazed at the breathtaking beauty of each person we meet, of each thing we see.

I prayed, "Come, Lord Jesus, transform all the areas of my inner universe. Come, Lord Jesus, take hold of each person, of everything, for they are rightly yours. You bought all at a high price some two thousand years ago. Come, Lord Jesus, send your Holy Spirit in abundance upon our earth that we might begin to see this glorious thing you made for us, reverence it, cherish it, draw out of everything and every person the loving goodness and beauty you have already hidden there. We are involved in a treasure hunt. We know where the treasure lies: in each person, in each thing. Often it is hidden by arrogance, selfishness and ignorance."

Because God is good, he revealed to me the secret beauty of the policeman who scowled furiously as I passed by with my cross shining in the sun. He revealed to me the beauty of many others.

The Great Leader appeared on television nearly every-day. I condemned him, judged him, rejected him, until one day God seemed to say in my heart, "I love him. He is my son. Are you without sin?"

It was easy to pray in the ten chapels of St. Basil's Cathedral, each one highly decorated by a huge iconostasis and numerous frescoes. Ivan IV, the Terrible, had it built (1554 to 1560) by a master architect. Each one of the ten chapels is topped by a different-type cupola, some in the form of domes, some onion-shaped, some tent-like. Their colors of gold, red, pink, green, white, orange, and the whole church reminded me not of this world but of the world to come when all things will be even more beautiful than St. Basil's. I heard that this glorious structure was named not after Basil the Great, but after *Basil the Fool.* If you know about him, please inform me.

In Russian spirituality the holy fool has always been highly honored as a very special image of Christ. Who was more of a fool than Jesus Christ, the Son of God, who made himself nothing, assuming the nature of a slave? "Let your bearing toward one another arise out of your life in Christ Jesus. For the divine nature was his from the first; yet he did not think to snatch at equality with God, but made himself nothing, assuming the nature of a slave. Bearing the human likeness, revealed in human shape, he humbled himself, and in obedience accepted even death— death on a cross. Therefore God raised him to the heights and bestowed on him the name above all names, that at the name of Jesus every knee should bow—in heaven, on earth, and in the depths—and every tongue confess, 'Jesus Christ is Lord,' to the glory of God the Father" (Phil 2:5-11).

In the Kremlin itself it was easy to pray in some of the world's most beautiful churches—now state museums. The Church of the Annunciation, the Church of the Assumption of Our Lady, the Church of St. Michael the Archangel, the Patriarchal Church of the Twelve Apostles. Thousands of people have worshipped God in these churches since the fourteenth century. They still do, quietly in their own hearts, as they listen to the guide's explanations.

I never found an irreverent guide in the whole of the Soviet Union. I remember in sorrow and in contrast the disdain of my guide in Avila, Spain, while we toured the churches and shrines dear to the memory of the great St. Teresa. Yes, strangely enough, my places of prayer, my sacred spaces where I met God, my personal temples of worship in Moscow were the Kremlin, the Red (beautiful) Square, and the Tretjakov Gallery where I joined the millions who had prayed before the icon of Our Lady of Vladimir and before Andrei Rublev's icon of the Loving Trinity.

In the afternoons I walked the streets of Moscow as a pilgrim, silently offering God's love to every person I met, and that includes thousands. The streets of Moscow are thick with people all hurrying somewhere.

One day I discovered the Soviet Union's best bookstore, "The House of Books" on Kallinin Avenue. The time had come to consider buying souvenirs to bring back home. I had seen magnificent postcards and decided to buy a whole lot of them as mementoes for my family, friends and benefactors. The postcards of Russia are utterly delightful, colorful, humorous, and often come in a series which tells a story. I would have loved to have brought home icon prints, especially of Our Lady of Vladimir and of the Trinity. I searched and hunted everywhere. There are no prints available, as far as I know. As mentioned before, I was most fortunate to discover a fine book of icons in a little store in Suzdal.

At the postcard counters two young women waited upon me with such care and concern that I could have sworn they belonged to a religious organization especially dedicated to assisting foreign clergy. Already overloaded with customers, they managed to take two or three minutes at a time to help me make a good selection. I bought hundreds of cards.

This kind of thing happened to me over and over again. I remember, for instance, walking into a Gastronom (food store) in Novosibirsk. Immediately, a gentleman in his early sixties, a customer like myself, came up to me and assisted me most courteously in making my purchases. I found that people on the whole treated me better when I wore my clericals than when I didn't. Young people under thirty often approached me to engage in some kind of conversation. I found them eager to hear about God, the outside world, religion and myself.

The guides everywhere kept insisting upon their atheism, their communism or at least their agnosticism. So did my Russian table companions in the fine Intourist restaurants. Yet, every time, they would ply me with searching questions on the reality of God and of the soul. "Do *you* really believe in God? Who is he to *you*? Are you sure there is a God? Why have you chosen a life of chastity? What value does it have?"

One day a smart, well-dressed and very intelligent woman close to forty was seated at my table by the head waiter. We made banal conversation for a few minutes.

Then she opened up with a barrage of religious questions, the likes of which I had never before been exposed to. She wanted answers and she wanted them then. For one and a half hours she questioned, and I tried to answer.

— "Did Jesus Christ really exist?"

— "He did."

— "Is it scientifically proven?"

— "His existence is more scientifically proven than the existence of any other man in history. His life has been investigated by thousands of scientists. The fact of his existence is as scientific a conclusion as anything Lenin ever reached."

— "What is the Trinity?"

— "It is the Father, the Son and the Holy Ghost."

— "Who are they?"

— "They are God."

— "How can three persons be one God? I find that hard to understand."

— "I believe it. I don't understand it."

— "Who is the Bogomater (the Mother of God)?"

— "Her name is Mary. Although a virgin, she gave birth to Jesus Christ two thousand years ago. She is called Bogomater because Jesus Christ is the second Person of the Holy Trinity. He is the Son of God and her Son."

— "How can a virgin bring forth a man and God?"

— "I don't know, but I believe it."

— "You are not fooling me, are you? This is the truth?"

— "Yes, this is the truth."

— "Thank you very much. I wish you the peace and love you wear on your cross."

People went out of their way to impress me with their atheism, simply, I suspect, because they were totally unsure of it themselves.

"Most young people here are atheists. Do the young people in Canada believe in God? Do they go to church?

What about in America? Do the young people there go to church?"

"Yes," I said, "the majority do. As a matter of fact, we in North America are undergoing a great spiritual revival. Thousands of young people during the last fifteen years have literally become 'Fools for Christ' (yuridivi). They leave their comfortable homes. They put on a cross or a rosary. They, as true pilgrims of the Absolute, walk the streets, the highways and byways of Canada and the United States. Some were called flower children; others hippies; others Jesus freaks. Many in their quest for God turned to the religions of the East—Buddhism, and especially Zen. Often they didn't know what they were looking for, but something in their hearts moved them to arise and go, like the pilgrims of old, seeking, seeking, ever seeking. Abraham is the pilgrim's ancestor. To him God spoke: "Now the Lord said to Abram, go from your country and your kindred and your father's house to the land that I will show you. And I will make of you a great nation, and I will bless you and make your name great, so that you will be a blessing. I will bless those who bless you, and him who curses you I will curse, and by you all the families of the earth shall bless themselves. So Abram went, as the Lord had told him" (Gen 12:1-4).

"Youth in North America is on the march, following Abraham. They also have heard the call of the holy. They will seek after the Absolute until they find him. Israel has always been on pilgrimage, listening to God, and following where he directs. Today the Catholic Church desires to be poor, to be a servant, to be a pilgrim people. We have no settled home here. We live in a little tent which the wind can blow away. Now we must build unshakable structures for the kingdom that never ends, a kingdom not made by hands, but by the Spirit of God. Our greatness is that we possess the love, the faith, the hope to build up the *glorious body of Christ*, and to prepare by love, with the help of the Holy Spirit of God, the day when all shall be 'One Christ loving himself.' "

Many countries have a Golden Legend, stories which tell of the glorious deeds attributed to their saints, to their heroes. There is the story of St. George and the dragon, which has captured the imagination of many races; of St. Christopher, the one who carried the little Christ across a river and found him immensely heavy; of St. Catherine of Alexandria, a beautiful eighteen-year-old maiden who loved Christ and refuted the arguments of all the great pagan philosophers of her day. Among the Russians, the most popular stories from the Golden Legend may possibly shock many Roman Catholics.

Every Saturday, so it goes, Our Lady descends into the hell of the damned. She brings them comfort and release from pain for 24 hours. On Holy Thursday she goes there to proclaim an amnesty from the Father which will last until Pentecost.

Many saints have prayed that somehow Lucifer and his followers might have a change of heart and be reconciled to the Father. Believe it or not, even some Roman Catholic saints did that. One of them, Charles Peguy, died at the Front in 1914, at the opening of World War I. These people put it very simply: "How can anyone be saved and enjoy eternal bliss if a single one of God's creatures is condemned and in pain?" No Council of the Holy Roman Catholic Church has decreed that it was wrong to pray for everyone's ultimate return to God, including Lucifer's. The Russians say that on the last day the Mother of Jesus, who is also the mother of the universe, will turn to her Son and intercede for all the condemned. What a glorious thing to contemplate. All men, all angels and devils reunited with each other, reconciled with the Father, praising, through the Holy Spirit, Jesus the Savior of All.

What a joy that will be!

13. SERGIUS TRINITY LAVRA TOWN: ZAGORSK

It was my last full day in Russia. I had gone to bed early the night before. Without setting my alarm I asked God to be awakened at seven, and that's what happened. At seven exactly I woke up, washed, shaved and dressed, excited at the day's prospects. At Mass time, in my very modest hotel room, my little missal fell open at the Mass in honor of the Guardian Angels. Each morning I considered it a great privilege to be allowed to praise, to intercede for the whole cosmos, to spread God's immense and powerful blessings over the Soviet Union with love and joy.

Promptly at eight, I entered the breakfast room and sat in "my chair," facing Lenin's tomb, the Spassky (the Savior's) Tower, which has served as entrance to the Kremlin on all solemn occasions for centuries. At the other end of the Beautiful Square stood St. Basil's Cathedral in all its glory. Two New York businessmen ate with me. They told me of their biggest disappointment: The local government's unwillingness to allow them to visit the country freely. I pointed out to them that all arrangements for travel in the Soviet Union must be made before you leave your own country. They were traveling on a business visa which allowed them to visit only the cities where they had business. It was interesting at breakfast to hear the tourists' reactions. I did my best to enlighten them and encourage them to drop their preconceived ideas. If it is true that in Rome you should do as the Romans do, let me assure you that it is infinitely more true in the Soviet Union.

The day was wet and drizzly. For an hour, I prayed the fifteen mysteries of the Rosary while walking up and down in front of the Intourist excursion office, waiting for my guide and chauffeur. Today would be a real day of pilgrimage.

At ten o'clock sharp, Svetlana, my guide, and Victor, the chauffeur, arrived. We introduced ourselves and were on our way to visit with *St. Sergius* in the Trinity Monastery (Lavra) in Zagorsk, some fifty miles northeast. We left Moscow via Mir Prospekt, that is, the *Avenue of Peace.* That thrilled me. Mir Prospekt was crowded with loaded trucks, the sure sign of a country that is building, building, building.

Industry is growing rapidly and many cities were heavily damaged during World War II. A great building boom is on. The immense wealth, mineral and otherwise, of Siberia is just beginning to be really exploited. The Soviets are eager, alert, enthusiastic, aggressive. There is so much to do, and employment for everyone. I was reminded of Canada and the United States during the years immediately following World War II. We too were cocky, assertive, sure of ourselves. We knew what there was to do and we were busy doing it. We thought we knew where we were going twenty-five years ago. But what a difference today! We suffer from grave indecision in the economy, in education, in the Churches! I wonder what mood will prevail in the Soviet Union at the turn of the century.

Such were my musings as we drove slowly between two lines of trucks. Svetlana pointed out the famous Soviet statue which symbolizes the union of worker and peasant: A young man, strong and virile, stretches forth with all his might holding high a hammer in his left hand. By his side, a healthy and eager young woman also strikes forward, holding the sickle in her right hand.

We passed by the modernistic monument to Soviet space conquests: a tall, curved, steel column whose sweeping, upward movement seems to propel into the sky the space capsule which sits on its top.

We glanced briefly at the seventy-nine pavilions of the Exhibition of Economic Achievement, another Soviet truimph.

In the heavy traffic, my side of the car was hit by a huge bus. Strangely enough our car didn't budge. Victor signaled the bus driver to stop. They both launched into a loud diatribe which got nowhere. Again we were on our way. I knew then why my missalette had opened up at the Mass of the Guardian Angels. I thanked them with joy.

Nowhere in the world, with the exception of the Holy Land, is there a road more traveled by Christian pilgrims than this one. Millions and millions of pilgrims have made the journey, generally on foot, from Moscow to the Trinity Lavra, since its foundation by St. Sergius in the middle of the fourteenth century. Peasants' houses cluster near each side of the way, for these peasants and their forebears had the immense privilege of providing hospitality, food and shelter to the numberless pilgrims. I could see, in my imagination, rows of men and women dressed in simple, humble, gray and black clothes, wearing a large icon on their breasts, using walking sticks, carrying, strapped around their shoulders, a little bag which contained a piece of bread, some salt, and perhaps a little clothing. I could "see" them walking in groups, or marching alone in deep, deep silence fingering their "Jesus beads." Every stone must be thoroughly impregnated with the "Jesus prayer" on this truly holy path.

Zagorsk is named after the Secretary of the Communist Party who was killed in 1919. Undoubtedly he rests in peace, for his name has now become synonymous with that which is most holy in Russia. Before 1919, Zagorsk was known as the Sergius Trinity Lavra Town (Troitsi Sergiev Lavra Passad). For centuries it had been strictly a monastery town. It is now a city of one hundred thousand people with many industries.

THE HUMBLED CHRIST IN RUSSIA

Let us talk about the man we have come to visit, St. Sergius (1314-1392). He is known in history and in the affection of the people as *"The Builder of Russia."* In 1337 he moved northeast of Moscow and founded a monastery dedicated to the Most Holy Trinity. He loved God passionately, and he loved Russia fervently. The Mongol-Tatars had pillaged and ruined his beloved country for centuries. The Russian princes warred against each other. Sergius, inspired by the Holy Spirit, knew exactly what to do to free his country from the oppressors, to unite the warring princes, and to gather all his countrymen under Moscow. He erected a *symbol* around which all could rally, the Church of the Most Holy Trinity. Thus he presented to his people the Holy Trinity as their model of union and as the only power which could change them and open their hearts to brotherly love.

It was destroyed by the Tatars in 1380. In 1420 it was rebuilt to serve a dual purpose: 1) to continue the unification of all Russia; 2) to house St. Sergius' remains. This church still stands, all white with a single cupola. Although of middle size, this edifice is the most powerful thing that has ever been built in Russia. Because of it, the princes became brothers. Because of it the Russian people rallied round their princes. Because of it the Tatars were gradually expelled or assimilated, beginning with the great victory of Kolikovo in 1380, which had been inspired by Sergius.

Sergius adopted for his monks the *hesychast* way of spirituality. The word *Hesychia* means something very simple, namely, *inner calm.* Its purpose is the *experience* of God, to know God at the center of one's being, not merely to know about God in one's head. This inner calm is acquired by repeating constantly the Jesus prayer, which takes many forms: "Lord Jesus Christ, Son of the Living God, be merciful to me a sinner"; "Lord Jesus, mercy"; "Jesus mercy."

This prayer, monotonous, repetitious, simple, uncompli-cated, reminds one of weaving. With it the Holy Spirit, source of all prayer, weaves within oneself a powerful cord with which one can descend slowly, gradually into God, who lives at the very center of ourselves. God manifests his presence eventually. He says, "I am here, and you are my beloved."

The cord can be weaved by the Holy Spirit and our Mother Mary only, of course, if we gently push aside our anxieties and the overwhelming desires which draw us away from God. Not all desires are detrimental to union with Him. In other words, our main work is to prevent our spiritual fingers from sticking to anything which is not from God.

Jesus Christ calls us sons of God, salt and light of the world, therefore glorious. St. Paul constantly reminds his Christians of their deep union with Christ and consequent, immense dignity. He tells them that animals and trees and minerals yearn to share in their glory. St. Peter fairly shouts to all Christians: "but you are a chosen race, a royal priesthood, a dedicated nation, and a people claimed by God for his own, to proclaim the triumphs of him who has called you out of darkness into his marvelous light. You are now the people of God, who once were not his people; outside his mercy once, you have received his mercy."

St. Sergius also lived and preached the continued transformation of every creature from darkness to ever-greater light, from coldness to ever-greater warmth and fire. He believed in cosmic salvation. Someday, through love, all would be fire and light as God is fire and light.

When a monk achieved peace, St. Sergius would say: "He has found his homeland, (motherland, "patrie," fatherland, country)." "Concentrate," he taught, "on what is enduring. Never let the moment's troubles overwhelm you. Like She-who-gave-birth-to-Christ, you are trans-figured by your fiat. Long for the parousia, the second coming of Christ, which already is present in your own heart, which already breaks forth for a few moments during the Divine Liturgy, which literally explodes at the Easter vigil." In such words he taught his monks, he rallied the Russians, he spread monasticism all over northeast Russia. Within a century after his death, one hundred fifty monasteries had been established in the area between Moscow and the White Sea.

Laymen and women by the thousands flocked to these monasteries to meet people who had touched God. They opened their hearts to them and asked for a healing, enlightening word from God.

St. Sergius, as St. Theodosius before him, had built his monastic life around the staretz. A monk would give himself for a number of years to the "Jesus prayer," manual labor, simple living, simple fare (they never ate meat or dairy products, but lived on fish, vegetables, grain, fruit) and discipline of the passions. When he had achieved a certain spiritual maturity, novices were entrusted to his care. He would become each young man's spiritual father. His method of training was extremely simple: "Do as you see me do."

The staretz had an immense spiritual influence all over Russia. To name a few: St. Cyril, St. Savva, St. Sossima near the White Sea, St. Stephen, who brought monasticism to Perm at the foot of the Ural Mountains, St. Tikhon of Zadonsk, who experienced a veritable parousia every Easter. One of my favorites, St. Seraphim of Sarov, lived only fifty miles west of the Trinity Monastery, at the beginning of the nineteenth century. He was confessor, spiritual director and advisor to some of the greatest men Russia ever produced: Gogol, Dostoyevsky, Tolstoy, Turgenev, etc.

While Moscow gradually became Russia's political center after 1380, the Trinity Lavra has always been its spiritual home. Even today, although the Patriarch officially lives in Moscow, he has a permanent residence in Zagorsk. The Moscow Theological Seminary there houses some two hundred students, and trains many more by correspondence. Through the centuries, the Trinity Lavra built large hostels for the pilgrims, and hospitals for the sick. Its thick walls served as a fortress and contain rooms to receive pilgrims. After the fall of Constantinople in 1453, Moscow and Zagorsk became the guardians of Orthodoxy for the whole world.

We left our car at the monastery gate. Briskly, Svetlana led me directly to the Church of the Most Holy Trinity. I can hardly describe what happened to me the moment the door closed behind us. On this muddy, Monday morning the church was comfortably full. People were praying with such devotion, such faith, such love that I felt carried up for a moment to the very feet of God, to the throne of Grace, to the very seat of Love. This seat, in my imagination, became none other than the glorious Virgin-Mary, carrying in her being Father, Son and Holy Ghost. Resplendent with their glory, on fire with their love, she seemed to sit close by and yet above the cosmos. From her heart, her hands, her face, shot forth blinding rays of light, sweetened by the blue rays of her own love. The minute I set foot in that church I was caught up. The parousia had indeed come. I told Svetlana, "Please sit down for a few moments, I simply have to pray."

A force drew me through the crowds directly to St. Sergius' resting place, a silver sarcophagus by a wall right in front of Rublev's exquisite Iconostasis. I joined the praying crowd around St. Sergius. If ever I prayed in my life, it was at that moment, as I prostrated before the Trinity. With all my heart I asked St. Sergius, I cried out to Our Lady of the Trinity, I implored Father, Son and Holy Spirit, to pour out all over Russia, all over the earth, all over the cosmos to the farthest star, the love, the pain, the prayers of Catherine de Kolyschkine, of Father Eddie Doherty, Father Callahan, of all the laymen, women and priests of our Madonna House family, of all the people living and dead who love Russia. For myself, I asked to be filled with St. Sergius' peace and love, and to share it with Catherine, our family and our friends. Three times I kissed his sarcophagus. I even lit a ruble candle ($1.25).

Try as I might, although I gazed and stared at the world's most beautiful Iconostasis standing right in front of me, to tell the truth, I couldn't see anything. My eyes and my heart were full of another scene, the glory of the Parousia. When I came down "from the clouds," I found Svetlana and sat by her for a couple of minutes to catch my breath. She herself, I think, was somewhat shaken. I led her to an icon which had caught my eye and asked her what it was. She answered, "Our Lady of Tikhvin." I remembered. Our Lady of Tikhvin is an honored miraculous icon. Mary points to her Son and says without words, "Follow him. He is the way." By the icon I prayed for a miracle. Then a funny thing happened.

I was facing the icon, and right in front of it, facing crossways, was a dear, fervent, Russian lady busy with her metanies (prostrations). I bent over the lady, trying to kiss the icon. The lady firmly took my foot and pushed it away. I stood there quietly, waiting. After each metanie she would glance up at me with a gleam in her eye, then immediately prostrate again. I kept waiting. At one point after some fifty metanies, she straightened her back for a second to rest it. I immediately went forward and got to kiss the miraculous icon. The lady looked at me and chuckled.

On our way out we met a priest who could speak a little English. I gave him some holy cards of Our Lady of Combermere and a short summary of the Madonna House

Apostolate founded by a Russian woman from Leningrad. I asked him to deliver it to the Patriarch with a special message of peace and love. As we parted, he said, "Let us pray with our whole hearts, all through our lives, that peace and love may come to all mankind during this century."

EPILOGUE: WHAT CAN STOP GOD?

Moscow was very hard on me at first, but, thank God, I came to love it. I felt the presence of the Evil One less there than I did in Paris, for instance. But I didn't spare the holy water or the blessings, and I prayed much more than I did in Paris. The love and prayers of thousands overflowed from my heart. I was also constantly aware of the silent springs of cool water: the loving, prayerful people who live in Russia, which daily wash the country clean, and refresh God's image in the leaders, the fifteen million Communists, and our two hundred fifty million Russian brothers and sisters.

The humiliati, the little ones of God, the anawim, bring hope and joy to those who suffer and hunger for freedom. Here, one is always aware of those who suffer the most, although they are never mentioned. One becomes convinced that nothing can stop God, no system, no police, no amount of repression. The people are returning to their roots, and rejecting some of the disorders that followed in the wake of the Communist revolution. People looked at my cross and wondered. Some smiled. Some got nervous. But all were amazed.

In many eyes I saw fear: "What if it is true? What if Christ did exist and is risen from the dead? What if I'm wrong? What if I've been deluded?"

This earth is being fed by secret springs: the blood of martyrs, the humility of the Church, the prayers of the little ones. How long can official, cold atheism survive all this warmth and love?

In 1943, Monsignor Fulton Sheen told me that the Russian people were the twentieth century's Suffering

110

Servant. "Some day," he said, "hundreds of Russians will come here to teach us how to be Christians." Karl Stern, one of the world's greatest psychiatrists, spoke along the same lines at a lecture given in Madonna House around 1960. Today these prophecies are coming true. Russian books of spirituality are becoming more influential in the West: *The Way of a Pilgrim, The Undistorted Image, The Art of Prayer*, and especially the books of Paul Evdokimov. More recently, the books of Archbishop Bloom and Catherine Doherty herself (*Poustinia*). Russian Orthodox spirituality indeed is making a major contribution to the West.

The flagship of that vast Russian fleet, Catherine Doherty, landed in America in 1921. Since then she has taught millions of little vessels to steer their course by *the* star—not the red star of Marxist Leninism, nor the purple one of Western materialism, but the bright white star of Christ's risen glory, his risen human body. Like Our Lady of the Way, Catherine points straight to Christ, and, because of her, millions know Christ, The Way. To him be glory and honor and praise for ever and ever and ever.

The morning of my departure, while thousands of tourists crowded the Kremlin, I planted a medal of Our Lady of Combermere there, asking her to bless, protect and heal all. Then I walked for one last time around the exterior walls of the Kremlin and of Red Square, encircling them with a final Rosary.

That afternoon, as the plane took off, my last view was of little villages, two rows of houses divided by a road. These little villages were where Russia's great men found God, the truth and themselves. The little villages where Russia was born, cherished and matured.

Oh Russia, God made of you a beautiful thing.

APPENDIX

MADONNA HOUSE—WHAT IS IT?

By: Catherine Doherty

Strange as this might seem—even in an article coming from the Foundress of Madonna House herself, the answer is not very clear.

It is not clear to me. It is not clear to our Staff Workers. And, of course, it may not be clear to you. The Lord truly means it when He says: "My ways are not your ways, nor My thoughts your thoughts."

Perhaps the simplest way would be to say that it is a Christian Community, or even better, a Christian Family of priests, laymen and women whom God brought together to preach the Gospel with their lives in the midst of our modern exploding, confused, questioning, fantastic, challenging world. Yes, it is a simple, humble, ordinary, loving Family which by its very existence proclaims the love of God for men and the love of men for God.

The members of Madonna House Apostolate dedicate their whole life to the forming and living of this family of Love, of which Christ is the Way leading directly to the Father with the help of the Holy Spirit.

Perhaps a better way of putting it would be: "The Apostolate of Madonna House and its members are pilgrims in this world, proclaiming the second coming of Christ when all things will be restored to him.

"Like all pilgrims, the members travel in poverty to find security only in Christ; journey in chastity to serve and love Christ in men; live in obedience to be concerned only with the Will of God."

Madonna House came to Combermere at the invitation of its Bishop to work in the Rural Apostolate. Three of us came, myself, Eddie Doherty, and Grace Flewwelling, a pioneer of our Apostolate. That was on May 17, 1947. Slowly, quietly we worked in this beautiful region; nursing, helping the needs of the community.

Just as slowly and constantly, men and women came to join us. They became part of our Apostolate. We are an Apostolate of laymen and women, and priests.

Eventually the influx of "vocations" demanded that we establish two separate entities in Madonna House. One, to continue to serve the countryside. We called that house St. Joseph's.

The other retained the name of Madonna House and became the Training Centre for those vocations!

During the summer months. . .June, July and August . . .we used to have a Summer School. We established a little Cana Colony for families. . .a camp about three miles away from Madonna House. People came to both. First in small numbers and then in an ever-growing torrent. Sometimes we had as many as two hundred, or possibly a few more, with the families and the children.

This went on until Vatican II, 1962.

It occurred to us that our Staff was working too hard at that time—those were the "building days."

The surge of vocations necessitated building dormitories and things like a laundry, a sewing room, office rooms, etc.

Those were also the days when our little Gift Shop was built, on sheer faith, with Our Lady as our sole "buyer."

I prayed very hard, since all this expansion called for money. The Gift Shop, incidentally, is the only one in Canada that exists, literally, on prayer.

Eventually a Handicraft Centre arose next to it.

Our "building," which so clearly bore marks of the Lord's will, took quite a toll of our staff.

It was also a time for field houses. At the present time we have mission houses in Whitehorse, Yukon; Edmonton, Alberta; Regina and Gravelbourg, Saskatchewan; Ottawa, Ontario; Stafford, Virginia; Winslow, Arizona; Carriacou, West Indies; Ellenburg, N.Y.; and Portland, Oregon.

Considering all these exciting things that were happening, plus the work and strain they entailed for our staff, I came up with an old Russian idea: "Poustinias."

What is a Poustinia! It is just a shack or cabin, where anyone can go to pray.

Our Poustinias are furnished with a table, a chair, a bed (no mattress, just wooden slats and two quilts), a Bible on the table, and a five-foot wooden cross without a corpus.

That, in my Russian mind, was a Poustinia, a little desert to which our staff were to come and rest in the Lord, praying and being refreshed whilst lifting up to Him the two arms of "prayer and penance." All you bring to that Poustinia is a loaf of bread and a thermos of coffee or tea, but preferably just water.

So far so good. I understood Madonna House. The staff understood Madonna House.

But suddenly, without the slightest warning, just after Vatican II, people began pouring in, individually and in groups. The hundreds became thousands.

Most of these were young. Priests came in great numbers too. Nuns likewise.

Madonna House is still a Training Centre for the young people who come to join us, to live our life of Poverty, Chastity and Obedience.

I have ceased to understand it; because the great number of people who come here, come seeking not *us*, exactly, but God Himself.

The count each year since has been approximately

3,500 young people, several hundred nuns, and a thousand priests!

We are delighted with the fact that they come. Our hospitality is wide open. Our house and our heart are there to welcome them. But we would like to clarify, to ourselves as well as to anyone else, that we are *NOT* a retreat center.

Although it is true that we have built several poustinias (due to the demands of priests, nuns and lay people), it is not a retreat house.

If anyone wants to come to Madonna House, we repeat, all are tremendously welcome. But they have to share the life of the family, which means they will have to get up in the morning at 6:30. Mass will be at 7:30, breakfast around 8:15. From there on, work needed for the community will be the business of the day.

At noon there is dinner and spiritual reading; then work again until four p.m. (in the summer 3:30). Then tea and then work again. Sometimes the work, when the need of the Apostolate demands it, goes on into the late hours of the evening with various "bees," collective effort in other words.

Those who want to spend time with us will participate in a new form of community living, with the possibility of spending twenty-four hours in one of our poustinias.

I don't know if I have explained what Madonna House is. It is so many things in one that I feel lost in trying to put it down on paper.

Yes, it is a Training Centre that by the grace of God and His will, has opened its doors and its heart wide to those who are seeking the Lord.

To all who wish to come, it offers a participation in its life-style and in its prayer-style. It is not a place that people might call a resting place, except in the sense that one "rests" in the heart of the Lord. It is a community whose only desire is to preach the Gospel with our lives.

Now have I clarified Madonna House? I still don't know. Maybe one has to come and see for himself. Come, but without any preconceived ideas.

Madonna House,
Combermere,
Ontario, KOJ ILO
Canada.